Praise for *The Nones*, second edition

Ryan P. Burge writes with a social-scientist's mind and a pastor's heart. *The Nones* is compellingly written and steeped in a wealth of data analyses, demonstrating the author's deep grasp of both the social reality and the religious importance of the people who identify themselves as atheists, agnostics, and "nothing in particular." The second edition adds significant insight into the impact of Covid-19 on the phenomenon and does a great job anticipating readers' questions as it moves through the data in a clear and convincing way.

—Kimberly H. Conger, professor of political science,
University of Cincinnati

Not only did Burge conduct groundbreaking research into this important social phenomenon, but he translates it into relevant and thought-provoking insights. As both a political scientist and pastor, there is no one better equipped to write about the future of American faith—or lack of it.

—Elle Hardy, author of *Beyond Belief: How Pentecostal Christianity Is Taking Over the World*

This second edition of *The Nones* is required reading for anyone attempting to make sense of America's religious landscape today. In this book, Ryan Burge skillfully takes his reader behind the curtain to examine complex data and social theory in an approachable, practical, and exciting way. Parsing out the nuances within broad religious identifiers, *The Nones* offers a road map for pastors, professors, field builders, and lay leaders to enter the public sector with confidence, compassion, and a greater awareness around who comprises our society, what they believe, and how we move forward together across lines of difference.

—Amar D. Peterman, founder, Scholarship for
Religion and Society

The Nones

The
Nones

Where They Came From,
Who They Are, and
Where They Are Going

Second Edition

Ryan P. Burge

FORTRESS PRESS
MINNEAPOLIS

THE NONES
Where They Came From, Who They Are, and Where They Are Going
Second Edition

Cover design: Kristin Miller
Cover image: © iStock 2020; Icon set of world religious symbols stock
illustration by Panya

Print ISBN: 978-1-5064-8824-0
eBook ISBN: 978-1-5064-8825-7

Contents

Preface to the Second Edition

I was sitting on a stool in front of a blackjack table in a dry lake bed about thirty minutes outside the Las Vegas strip. Looking around I saw nothing but solar panels, high tension electrical lines, and eight members of a television production crew, most of whom I had met when we arrived at the location for the shoot. All because I wrote a book about the increasing number of people with no religious affiliation.

This whirlwind of events that brought me to the Nevada desert had started five days earlier when I received an email from Mike Rubens, a correspondent for the television show *Full Frontal with Samantha Bee*. He was interested in the changing religious composition of the United States and had found my name after a quick Google search. We chatted on the phone for about an hour on Monday afternoon, and by Friday I was on a plane to Las Vegas to do a face-to-face interview with Mike in one of the most desolate places I had ever been.

The segment was Mike's attempt to try to understand how and why American religion had changed so significantly in such a short period of time. Between snippets of conversation around the blackjack table were clips of Mike interviewing inebriated people on the Las Vegas strip about the last time they went to church. The show aired in November 2021 and it seemed like an out-of-body experience when I saw my face on television.

I never intended to become the go-to expert on the demographics of disaffiliation. I just wanted to put all the graphs I had made about those without religious affiliation (nones) in a single place. But somehow *The Nones* has struck a chord with Americans from all walks of life and a variety of faith backgrounds. As soon as the book was released, I was asked to give talks to diverse groups of people about the future of American religion. One day, I shot a short piece for the Christian Broadcasting Network in the morning, and then appeared on a podcast for the Freedom From Religion Foundation in the afternoon. By pure happenstance, I managed to write about a topic that was in the middle of the cultural zeitgeist and people were eager to learn more about the changing religious landscape.

Over the course of dozens of media appearances, I began to understand that reporters were not just reaching out to me because of the book but also because of my personal background. As I explain in the first few pages of *The Nones,* I am both an academically trained social scientist *and* a pastor in the American Baptist Church. People in the media found that combination fascinating. I can't tell you how many times I've been asked what it's like to be a political scientist and a pastor. I respond the only way I know how: "It doesn't seem odd to me because I've been doing both jobs for my entire adult life, and I don't know anything else."

Wearing both hats puts me in some uncomfortable positions from time to time. There have been countless times during an interview where a reporter will ask me a question and I have to reply, "Do you want me to answer that question as a social scientist or a pastor?" Usually, they say that they want me to answer as both. While living at the intersection of these two very different careers has been a tremendous asset when it comes to writing about politics and religion, it doesn't come without its pitfalls.

For instance, lots of atheists and agnostics accuse me of writing *The Nones* to provide practical advice to Christians on how to proselytize more effectively to people without a religious affiliation. They see my work as nothing more than an evangelistic tract with a few charts and graphs. At the same time, when I get feedback from pastors and denominational leaders about *The Nones,* they often tell me that they wish I would provide more actionable advice on how churches can reach the nones. It's really put me in a no-win situation.

That's part of the impetus for writing a second edition of *The Nones*. I wanted to expand on the parts of the book that are more academically focused while also spending some more time providing insights for religious individuals trying to reach out to those people who have no religious affiliation. Instead of leaning harder on one part of my personal background, I want to continue to try to speak to the nones and the somes all at the same time.

The other reason that I wanted to update *The Nones* is because so much has changed since I wrote the first edition just a few years ago. In that version, the data that I was using stopped in 2018. Now, I have access to surveys that were collected as late as the spring of 2022. During that short four-year time period, the share of Americans who have no religious affiliation rose by at least five percent. That increase represents nearly fifteen million new adults—a sum that is larger than the Southern Baptist Convention, the largest Protestant denomination in the United States.

Beyond updating the data in the previous version of *The Nones*, I also wanted to tackle a question that often comes up in daily conversations I am having with reporters, pastors, and casual observers: What did the global pandemic do to American religion? In mid-March 2020 there were fewer people gathering in houses of worship across the United States than on any other weekend in at least a hundred years. Many people who had been regular attendees for decades didn't step foot in a sanctuary for months. Others hadn't darkened a church door for many years. The lockdowns gave these people a chance to slow down and consider their purpose in life, as well as their connection to the Divine. The second edition of *The Nones* is my attempt at quantifying the impact that COVID-19 had on the rise of the nones and the shifting shape of American religion.

If I've learned anything through writing *The Nones*, it's simply this: people want to be able to make sense of the world around them. They read the news every day and take notice of things that are happening, but they aren't exactly sure why those things are happening. Giving readers a broad framework to understand where America was a few decades before and then describing the current state of affairs can be an incredibly valuable exercise. I hope this new edition of *The Nones* will give more people a mental scaffolding that provides structure and order in their understanding of the world.

Preface to the First Edition

Two facts will help place this book in a proper context. I have been pastoring American Baptist churches for the past fifteen years, and I also have a PhD in political science, having published fifteen articles in peer-reviewed academic journals. What that means is that I have constantly straddled the world of faith and academia. I realize that makes me pretty atypical. I'm no fun at dinner parties because I refuse to talk about my work—as a pastor or an academic—in a social setting. Way too many landmines. But it does make me pretty well suited to present data about American religion to pastors.

More specifically, I think it makes me an ideal voice to write about one of the most important shifts that has occurred over the last forty years in American religion: the rise of the religiously unaffiliated. As a pastor who is also an academic, I have firsthand knowledge of the power of statistics for people of faith. I have written dozens of pieces for *Christianity Today*, Religion News Service, and Barna Group that are all grounded in data and receive an overwhelmingly positive response from a variety of audiences.

Unfortunately, as powerful as statistics are, I can't tell you how many sermons I've heard, books I've read, and tweets I've seen in the past few years from well-meaning pastors that are just not statistically accurate. Pastors are supposed to be in the business of preaching the Truth (about not only Jesus Christ but also the social world), but a lot of them need to stay in their lane.

Let me be clear: I don't blame pastors for wanting to use statistics to try to make a point about how church membership is in decline and the religiously unaffiliated are becoming an increasingly important factor in American religion. Pastors want to leave their flock with one thing they can discuss when they sit down for lunch after church, and a good data point sticks in the brain in a way few other things do. People want to have unbiased facts explained in a way that they can understand. Pastors need to be steady sources of accurate information, but unfortunately, some of them aren't taking the time to fact-check everything that goes into the weekly sermon.

However, one of the most valuable things I learned in graduate school was how little I—and all of us—know about most of the world, which is why data in untrained hands can be a dangerous thing. Just as I wouldn't want one of my political science colleagues to try to explain the evolution of Trinitarian thought in Protestant Christianity, I don't want pastors to try to explain how Karl Marx thought about religion or expound on the implications of internet-based polling.

At the same time that I learned to be humble about what I don't know, I also learned to speak confidently in areas to which I have devoted years of study. Charting the course of American religion for the past five decades has been my life's work up to this point. Still, being a quantitative social scientist as well as a pastor often puts me in an awkward position. Sometimes I am asked to present my work to denominational leaders. Inevitably during the question-and-answer time, someone in the audience will bring up a particularly thorny topic and want me to weigh in on it. I almost always preface my response by asking, "Would you like me to answer that as a pastor or as a quantitative social scientist?"

In this book, I try to do both. I live in the data, creating charts and graphs almost every day. But in between recoding variables and specifying regression models, I carve out time to work on my sermon or visit one of my members in the hospital. My focus over the last few years has been twofold: publishing enough to earn tenure at my university and helping pastors and denominational leaders understand the world around them a bit better. My goal is to take all the education I have had in the social sciences to make the theory comprehensible and the data accessible. So, pastors and committed lay leaders, consider this book a resource to get it right when talking about American religion—a little cheat sheet for your work.

Introduction

It all started with a tweet.

A lot of social scientists I follow on social media were noting that the General Social Survey (GSS) had just released the raw data from the 2018 wave, and scholars were already cranking out quick analyses of some of the top-line changes in American political and religious life. For social scientists who study religion, the GSS is the most important survey instrument for analyzing changes in American society. It's the gold standard for measuring religious change in America. That's largely because the GSS has been asking the same religion questions in essentially the same way since its creation in 1972. If a researcher wants to know what share of Americans never attended church in the 1980s, the GSS is the place to go. As soon as I read the news, I immediately downloaded the cumulative data file and started doing some analysis.

My primary objective was simple. I wanted to know how the seven major religious traditions in the United States had shifted over the previous two years. I had already published several pieces about religious measurement, so I had all the code I needed stored on my hard drive. All I had to do was run it on the updated data file and visualize the results. But by the time I had gotten home from work, my two boys needed dinner and a bath. I could hardly contain myself, so I moved quickly. As soon as both of them had filled their bellies with peanut butter and jelly and were happily playing in a bubble bath, I bounded down the stairs to my office and ran the more than two hundred lines of computer code that would calculate the size of all seven religious traditions in every survey year of the GSS dating back to the early 1970s.

And I saw it immediately.

The percentage of religiously unaffiliated people had steadily risen since the early 1990s. Previously, the "nones" had zoomed past 10 percent of the population by 1996, crossed the 15 percent threshold just a decade later, and managed to reach 20 percent by 2014. That rise had not abated in 2018. It had finally happened: the nones were now the same size as both Roman Catholics and evangelical Protestants. That meant that the religiously unaffiliated were statistically the same size as the largest religious groups in the United States.

I had to let the world know, but I was on a time crunch. My boys were starting to get restless in the bathtub. So I quickly put together a graph, picked a premade color scheme, and added the names of each religious tradition to the visualization. I wrote up a quick caption, noted that there was "some big news" about the religiously unaffiliated, and hit the tweet button.

I went back upstairs to get my boys ready for bed, helped them get pajamas on, brushed their teeth, and read a quick bedtime story before lights-out. Then I looked down at my phone. The graph had already been retweeted nearly a hundred times. It was going viral.

What followed was one of the busiest periods of my life. Before this, I had spoken to two or three reporters in my entire academic career; now I was fielding two or three interview requests per day. That one simple graph took on a life of its own. It was picked up by most major media outlets in the United States, including the *New York Times* and the *Washington Post*, and it landed on the front page of CNN's website. Reporters from Europe were intrigued, and the story ended up in the *Times* and the *Daily Mail*. It made the front page of Reddit, receiving over thirty-six thousand upvotes and over two thousand comments. I appeared on C-SPAN on Easter Sunday.

Journalists, podcasters, and pastors were all asking me the same questions: How did this happen? And what does this mean for the future of American religion? I didn't know it at the time, but my entire life had led me to this moment.

My career path has been a bit unusual. While I have been a quantitative social scientist for over a decade, I have also been in Christian ministry since just after my twentieth birthday. Wrestling with questions about the future of American religion is not just some cold and calculated academic exercise for me. It's something I experience every Sunday when I get behind the pulpit.

I grew up Southern Baptist. My mother was a Sunday school teacher and my father drove the church bus. My grandmother was the church secretary, and my grandfather was an usher. We went to church every time the doors were open. I was the kid who was there every Sunday morning and Sunday night. When I entered junior high, the youth group of First Baptist Church of Salem, Illinois, became my home away from home. I went to as many church camps, youth rallies, spaghetti fundraisers, and lock-ins as I could. As I moved into high school, I began to lead Bible studies for the younger kids. I was all in.

During the spring of my sophomore year of college, I was confronted with a problem. I didn't have a summer job lined up. Through a series of seemingly random events, I became aware that a church just twenty miles from my hometown wanted a youth ministry intern for the summer. I applied, was interviewed, and accepted the job at the tender age of twenty. I had no idea what I was doing. That three-month internship turned into a three-year position that I left only after I decided I wanted to pursue a graduate degree in political science. In graduate school, I began pastoring a small church of about thirty retirees. A year later, I was called by First Baptist Church of Mt. Vernon, Illinois. Fifteen years later, I am still behind the pulpit. I constantly wonder how all this happened.

While at First Baptist, I finished a master's thesis, got married, bought a house, defended my dissertation, and had two children. And my church went from having about fifty people in the pews to just over twenty. What was happening in American religion was also happening right in front of me.

This book is an effort to understand and explain how the number of religiously unaffiliated went from no more than a rounding error to about thirty percent of the US population. While others have tried to make these seismic changes about doctrine and dogma, that's not the approach I will be taking. Instead, I will use both the theory and methodological tools put forth by social science to explore what demographic, religious, and political factors have given and are giving rise to the nones.

My work is unapologetically quantitative. That means you will find a lot of charts and graphs throughout these pages. Here's why I think that's essential: no one can accurately conceptualize what American religion looks like today, let alone what it looked like thirty years ago. We all live in our own social, cultural, and religious bubbles. The human mind often clings to anecdotes that represent the extreme cases, not the average ones. It's nearly impossible for any one individual to have a high-level view of American religion. While surveys are not foolproof (and we will discuss some of their flaws in just a few pages), they are one of the only ways to generate an objective assessment of people's beliefs and behavior over time.

If you are scared off by math, there's nothing to fear. I have taken great care to present simplified visualizations that are not based on complicated statistical models. More often than not, I am just doing simple arithmetic. A lot of social scientists seem to forget how much we can learn by simply counting things. However, if you are still struggling to understand a graph, the text will explain the visualization. I am going to point out findings you may have missed, and I will use the text to provide some additional information about the visualization.

The data for this work comes from a variety of sources that I have collected and organized over the course of my academic studies. Two primary surveys will appear frequently. The aforementioned GSS is an invaluable resource when looking at religious trends that stretch back for decades. However, the smaller sample size of the GSS can create problems related to statistical uncertainty. The Cooperative Election Study (CES) is huge in comparison. While the 2016 wave of the GSS contained about three thousand respondents, the CES conducted in the same year had a total sample size of sixty-four thousand. Despite its tremendous survey sample, however, the CES suffers from one major problem: it was not created until 2006. Therefore, doing long-term trend analysis is not possible.

The structure of the book is as follows: the first chapter is a deep dive into the seven religious traditions that are identified by scholars of American religion. I describe each tradition in broad strokes and track the change in its size over the past four and a half decades. Explaining why the religiously unaffiliated have risen in the United States is the aim of the second chapter. Topics of discussion here include grand theories of social science, issues with survey methodology, and the rise of the internet. The next section of the book will be focused on sketching the outlines of the three types of religious nones: atheists, agnostics, and those who identify as nothing in particular. In this new edition, I've added a chapter about the impact that the global pandemic has had on American religion—it's something I am asked about constantly. Finally, the book will end with a discussion of the future of American religion. My aim here is to direct pastors and denominational leaders to think about ways to respond to the rise of the nones by understanding which factors can't be changed in American society and which ones can.

One of the lessons I try to impart to my students is that the role of a social scientist is not to describe the world as we wish it were, or hope it could be, but instead to describe it as it actually exists. That's my goal here. The data will be my guide, and providing simple and clear explanations will be my focus. I am reminded of the words of St. Paul when he wrote, "For now we see in a mirror, dimly" (1 Cor 13:12). It's my hope that after this book, the mirror will be slightly more illuminated.

CHAPTER 1

What Does the American Religious Landscape Look Like?

It's always amazing to me how people spend thousands of hours and millions of dollars on just classifying things. For instance, in late 2018, scientists from more than sixty countries around the globe met in Versailles, France, faced with an unbelievably important problem: defining how much a kilogram weighed. The reference measure was literally a block of metal that was held under glass. The International Bureau of Weights and Measures chose that hunk of material to be a kilogram, a reference that is used untold millions of times a day around the globe. But they were facing a problem—the kilogram no longer weighed a kilogram. It was losing its mass very slowly over time. The reference was no longer accurate, and science had to make a change. They eventually adopted a resolution to move to a more precise and consistent measurement.[1]

In the United States, there's an entire industry that has cropped up called "tariff engineering." Those who engage in this practice try to convince the United States Court of International Trade that a raw material, a children's toy, or any other item imported into the country should be placed in a different classification in the US tax code. For instance, several costume companies sued the federal government because some of the higher-end Santa Claus suits that they had imported were being taxed as "fancy dress" instead of a "festive costume," which resulted in their having to pay millions of dollars in additional taxes to the government. After a two-year legal process, the court ruled that the Santa Claus suits were, in fact, "fancy dress" and must be taxed at the higher rate.[2]

Being a researcher who studies American religion often feels like being a tariff engineer or a scientist trying to decide what a kilogram actually means—except in our case, the hunk of metal or expensive Santa costume actually has very strong opinions about its place in the world as well. It's like trying to define a bowl of gelatin after it has been mixed and as it sits in the refrigerator; by the time you have come to a consensus on a term for the bowl of neon-green soup, it's become something else entirely.

That's not to say that social science hasn't done its best to try to nail down a definition of religious affiliation, because it has. Beginning in the 1990s, a group of political scientists who were pioneering the study of American religion and politics began to articulate a classification scheme that became known as "the three Bs": religious behavior, religious belief, and religious belonging. (It bears noting that several of the authors of this typology were themselves evangelical Protestants and so had likely sat through hundreds of sermons that were structured around three central points that all began with the same letter of the alphabet.) Each of the Bs has its own set of theoretical and methodological strengths and weaknesses.

THE THREE BS

Behavior

Religious behavior is tangible evidence of an individual's faith. For instance, it takes no leap in logic to assume that someone who attends church several times a week is likely to be more religious than an individual who attends only when she visits her grandmother every few years. However, church attendance is not the only dimension on which social scientists measure religious behavior. Things like how frequently an individual prays, how often or how much they donate to their church, or if they try to convert their friends and neighbors to their flavor of religion are all forms of religious behavior.

From a social science standpoint, using church attendance as a measure of religiosity makes sense. If someone says that they are Catholic but attend mass only once a year, they will be much less likely to be exposed to the theology and the religious culture of Catholicism than someone who is a faithful weekly attender. On the other hand, religious behavior, especially church attendance, is not without its deficiencies. For instance, many incredibly devout elderly people are physically unable to attend services (or were unable to meet in person because of pandemic restrictions), which means that they would score lower on a religiosity index. Another issue with using religious behavior to rate religious devotion is that some religions place a greater emphasis on attendance than others. For instance, evangelical and Mormon culture strongly encourage it, but it is not so important among Hindus or Buddhists. Also, religious behavior measures may undercount people who have moved to a new area and haven't found a church where they feel comfortable yet, or people who have young children whom they may not want to fight to keep quiet during a worship service.

Belief

Religious belief is what most people think about when they are asked to describe the goal of religion. I have heard many people state very forcefully that there is only one real reason to go to church and that is to strengthen one's relationship with the divine. This viewpoint presupposes a faith that is completely vertical in orientation—that faith is about an individual's relationship with God—and largely writes off the relationship one can have with other people in the congregation. From this perspective, the way an individual thinks is the most important dimension for social scientists to measure; it's a psychological understanding of religion. The question most often used to measure religious belief relates to an individual's view of a holy text. For instance, the General Social Survey (GSS) asks respondents which of three statements comes closest to describing their thoughts about the Bible:

- The Bible is the actual word of God and is to be taken literally, word for word.
- The Bible is the inspired word of God but not everything in it should be taken literally word for word.
- The Bible is an ancient book of fables, legends, history, and moral precepts recorded by men.

Biblical literalism has become a proxy for a whole host of conservative religious beliefs. However, this measure is also incredibly problematic. The primary reason is that it is biased against people who don't practice Protestant Christianity. While there are many devout Catholics in the United States, the official position of the Catholic Church is not biblical literalism but instead that the Bible should be interpreted in light of the church's teachings on different theological issues. Therefore, many theologically conservative Catholics do not classify themselves as literalists and are thus not counted as having high levels of religiosity, although they might be very religious by other measures. In addition, dozens of other faith groups—including Jews, Muslims, and those of Eastern faith traditions—have a difficult time answering a question about the Bible. While other questions have been used to measure an individual's religious belief, like asking about the existence of Satan, an afterlife, or evil in the world, many of them fall prey to the same issues that plague the question about biblical literalism: they are specific to one type of Christianity.

Belonging

The final *B* is that of religious belonging, which is the one that will be used as the unit of analysis in the remainder of this chapter. One of the primary problems that social science has to face is this: How do people know who they are and what they are about? That is, how do people orient themselves in social space? How do they define who may be friendly and who could potentially be hostile? One way people do this is by setting down markers, both visible and invisible, denoting what types of groups they want to affiliate with and what groups they see as undesirable. Think about someone who wears a camouflage shirt even when they are not going out to hunt. Or a man who wears a suit and tie to a wedding where others are wearing blue jeans. Some people proudly display their political affiliation on the bumper of their car, while others make it clear who they voted for by the content they share on their Facebook page. These are subtle ways for people to signal to others who they are and what type of people they would like to associate with.

A social scientist who uses religious belonging to sort people into categories does so based on the notion that religion is a decidedly social affair and that choosing a religious group is an intentional way of anchoring oneself in the social, religious, and political world in which they live. The preeminent political scientists Larry Bartels and Christopher Achen contend that people's driving principle as they move through life is, "What would people like me" do in a given situation?[3] That includes at the ballot box, in the pews, or on social media. If this is the proper way to understand the social world, then the primary question that social science has to answer is, How do individuals pick who is "like them"? I would argue that religion is an ideal way, an incredibly visible one, for citizens to orient themselves as part of the social world.

Consider this: there may be no more easily malleable demographic factor in American life than one's religious affiliation. For the vast majority of Americans, concepts like race and gender are incredibly concrete and fixed. For most, education is a pursuit that occurs only during a short period of their lives. And while one's income can drastically fall due to downsizing or recession, that usually is not followed by a drastic change in social or political behavior. Age is obviously a function of time. Other things like a change in marital status may happen once or twice, and people become parents just a handful of times.

Religion doesn't work like that. None of the demographic factors just mentioned can be changed as easily as religious affiliation. As an example, consider someone who took a survey a year ago and noted that they were Presbyterian, but when they were asked the same question about religion this week, they indicated that they had no religious affiliation. Did their actual religious behavior change dramatically between last year and now? More than likely, the answer is no. What is more plausible is that they were rarely attending services before but still clung to that religious identity. But for reasons that can never be completely understood, they made the conscious choice to say in the most recent survey that they have no current religious affiliation. It required not a conversation with their pastor or a public pronouncement to their friends and family but instead just a subtle shift in their mind: from seeing themselves as a Protestant Christian to someone who has no attachment to any religious group. That one simple shift can be indicative of a tremendous amount of change in the way that a person thinks about their place in the world.

So how do social scientists sort the menagerie of religious affiliations into categories that are not so broad that they lose all conceptual clarity or so large that they would be impossible to easily remember? The most widely adopted system in use today is called RELTRAD. It was developed by a team of social scientists two decades ago as a way to sort individuals in the GSS into different religious classifications. It's fair to say that no one, including the creators of RELTRAD, loves the classification scheme. However, its usage has become pervasive in American social science, with dozens of peer-reviewed books and articles using the typology every year. It's the best that we have.

Here's how it works. It takes a series of questions about religious affiliation in the GSS and places each specific religious tradition in one of seven categories: evangelical Protestant, mainline Protestant, Black Protestant, Catholic, Jewish, observant of other faith traditions, and nonaffiliated. These seven categories are what I will discuss in some detail in the remainder of this chapter. But first, I wanted to provide a broad sense of what American religion has looked like over the past forty-six years.

Before we move on to the graphs, a quick aside. The General Social Survey is usually conducted biannually, in even-numbered years. This means that there should be GSS data from 2020. However, that did not happen. The global pandemic threw a real curveball to the team that administers the GSS, because it has traditionally been conducted in a face-to-face environment. Given the restrictions on public gathering, the GSS had to switch gears and move to an online administration. This delayed putting the survey in the field until 2021 but also had a tremendous impact on the results of the 2021 GSS when it comes to religious affiliation. I will describe these changes in greater detail in chapter 5. Because of the aberrations in the 2021 data, the graphs visualized here will end in the last year of the typical GSS administration in 2018.

In broad terms, the graph in figure 1.1 shows two dominant religious traditions: evangelical Protestants and Catholics. Three traditions are smaller: Black Protestants, observants of other faith groups, and Jews. And finally, there are two traditions that have had a great

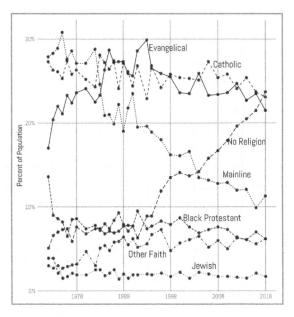

Figure 1.1. American religion from 1972 to 2018.

Data from the General Social Survey, a project of the independent research organization NORC at the University of Chicago, with principal funding from the National Science Foundation, https://gss.norc.org/Get-The-Data.

deal of volatility over the past four and a half decades: mainline Protestants and those without a religious affiliation—the nones, as I call them. While this book is focused on those who claim that they have no connection to a faith tradition, it's important to understand what options are available to people who desire to join a religious community—before they check the "none of the above" box. Some may be selecting the "no religion" box because they feel as if they have no better options on the survey. It's crucial to understand what those other options are. To that end, what follows is a brief discussion of some of the major features of these seven groups as well as an explication of how their share of the American population has shifted over the past forty-six years. This is by no means an exhaustive description of these groups, but I hope it will serve as an entrée into picturing American religion through a wide lens.

THE SEVEN RELIGIOUS TRADITIONS
IN THE UNITED STATES

Evangelical Protestants

It's fair to say that when the average American thinks about Protestant Christianity, they likely conjure up images of evangelicals. However, the term *evangelical* itself is hotly debated by scholars and laypeople alike. In just the past few years, there has been fierce discussion among historians, social scientists, and theologians about what it actually means.[4] The RELTRAD scheme classifies several denominational groups as evangelical. The largest is the Southern Baptist Convention, which is also the largest Protestant denomination in the United States, with 13.7 million members in 2021.[5] Other traditions classified as evangelical include the Assemblies of God (as well as other Pentecostal traditions), the Free Methodist Church, and the Lutheran Church—Missouri Synod. In addition, most people who say that they attend a nondenominational church are also placed in the evangelical category. The race of churchgoers is taken into account as well. For instance, Black Southern Baptists are classified as Black Protestants, not evangelicals. That means that this tradition is overwhelmingly, but not exclusively, white.

Speaking theologically, evangelicals hold to a conservative view of the Bible. In the past decade, the share of evangelicals who believe that the Bible is the literal word of God has hovered between 55 and 65 percent. A majority of these churches do not allow women to become pastors. Instead, they practice what has been called "complementarianism," an interpretation of the Bible that indicates the genders are equal yet complement each other through their use of different skill sets. This complementarian view is most apparent in the fact that women are not permitted to be pastors in evangelical churches. Additionally, a hallmark of evangelical theology is its emphasis on a born-again experience. This is described as a dramatic, often emotional moment when an individual gives themselves over to the call of God and the Holy Spirit enters their heart. The result of this event is expected to be a transformation in belief and behavior.

It's impossible to talk about evangelicals without a discussion of their politics. For example, the fact that 81 percent of white evangelicals voted for Donald Trump in 2016 and 2020 has been widely reported by those in the media.[6] However, what many reports miss is that four in five white evangelicals also voted for the Republican candidates for president in both 2008 and 2012. The close kinship between evangelicals and the GOP dates back to the formation of the religious right by a small group of influential evangelical pastors in the late 1970s. Many of them began to espouse a message of free markets, low taxes, and social conservatism. Abortion and gay marriage have persisted as the key issues for many evangelicals, with two in three evangelicals opposing abortion and same-sex marriage in 2016.

As can be seen in figure 1.2, the trend line for evangelicals over the past forty-six years serves as an interesting litmus test for those who try to interpret the data. One set of responses is typically along the lines of "Look how far evangelicals have fallen in the last twenty-five years." This perspective is rooted in comparing the high-water mark for evangelicals in 1993, 30 percent, to their current share of the population, 22 percent. That's an eight-percentage-point decline in

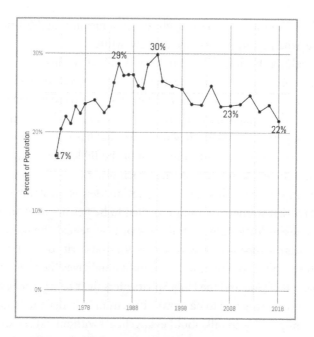

Figure 1.2. Evangelicals from 1972 to 2018.

Data from the General Social Survey, a project of the independent research organization NORC at the University of Chicago, with principal funding from the National Science Foundation, https://gss.norc.org/Get-The-Data.

two and a half decades. But there's another way to look at this data: that the period from 1983 to 2000 was somewhat of an outlier. If those years are eliminated, then evangelicals have basically held the same share of the population for the entire forty-six years. However, it's also accurate to say that evangelicals have seen an erosion in their share of the population since the beginning of the millennium. Their share has declined by about two percentage points in twenty years—a small amount, but one that may be worrisome for evangelicals.

Mainline Protestants

While evangelicals are the conservative form of American Christianity, mainline Protestants are perceived as the more moderate flavor. Their name comes from the fact that many of these churches were built on the main streets of towns and cities across the country. The largest denominations are often called the "Seven Sisters": the United Methodists, the Evangelical Lutheran Church in America, the Presbyterian Church (USA), the Episcopal Church, the American Baptist Church, the Disciples of Christ, and the United Church of Christ. While many of these church denominations are relatively new, they often trace their history back hundreds of years. For instance, the modern Episcopal Church finds its roots in North America in the early 1600s, when the Church of England was the official church of the Virginia colony.[7] Mainline Protestants are also largely white and are rapidly aging; the average mainline Protestant was nearly sixty years old in 2018.

As previously hinted at, mainline Protestants occupy the middle ground in matters of theology. They aren't as liberal as Unitarians, for instance, but their view of the Bible is not as strict as that of their evangelical brethren. While nearly two in three evangelicals are biblical literalists, just one in three mainline Protestants believes that the Bible should be read literally. Mainline denominations are also open to having women in the pulpit. In fact, that may be the touchstone of mainline Protestantism—a belief in "egalitarianism," which contends that women and men were created equal and therefore should have the same opportunities in ministry. Several of these denominations also support same-sex marriage. For instance, the United Church of Christ allowed couples of the same sex to wed as early as 2005.[8]

People often assume that because mainline Protestants are more religiously liberal, they should also side with the Democrats at the ballot box. However, the reality is often more complicated than that. Some of these traditions do lean to the left. For instance, nearly six in ten members of the Disciples of Christ identify with the Democrats, along with simple majorities in the Episcopal Church, the American Baptist Church, and the United Church of Christ. However, 56 percent of the largest mainline denomination in the United States, the United Methodist Church, are Republicans; just 34 percent are Democrats.[9] Often this partisan affiliation has more to do with economic issues than social topics, however. Mainline Protestants are typically white-collar workers who enjoy higher incomes and therefore want to see lower tax rates and less government bureaucracy.

While evangelicals have had a roller-coaster pattern of growth and decline, the mainline trajectory has almost entirely been downward, as can be seen in figure 1.3. A statistic that always stands out to me is that from 1972 until 1983 the largest religious tradition in the United States was mainline Protestant Christianity. In fact, none of the other seven religious traditions in the past forty-six years has crept above 30 percent of the population—except for mainline Protestants, who made up 31 percent of Americans in 1976. However, in a span of just twelve years, mainline Protestants lost a third of their members, dropping to just 19 percent in 1988. Since then, the decline has slowed somewhat. By 2004, they were below 15 percent and then in 2016 fell even further, to 10 percent of the population. They have seen a small rebound in 2018; however, that may be just an aberration in the data.

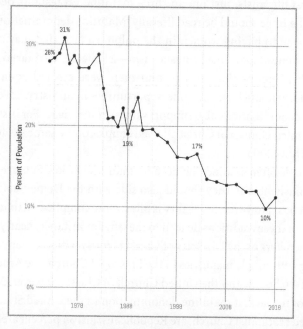

Figure 1.3. Mainline Protestants from 1972 to 2018.

Data from the General Social Survey, a project of the independent research organization NORC at the University of Chicago, with principal funding from the National Science Foundation, https://gss.norc.org/Get-The-Data.

Black Protestants

The final type of Protestant to consider is those who attend historically Black churches in the United States. The fact that an entirely different category is needed just because of the color of a worshipper's skin makes many people bristle at first blush. However, there are solid historical, social, and political reasons to separate Black Protestants. Many of those are rooted in the history of slavery and Jim Crow, as well as the racial discrimination that persists in America today. Even after the Civil War, freed Black Americans were not afforded the same rights and access to social organizations as their white neighbors. Because of that isolation, the Black church evolved into an entirely different type of institution from white Protestantism.

If white Christians wanted to join a social club, they could simply become members of the Lions or the Rotary or the American Legion. They would be embraced with open arms, and these clubs provided a network of connections to people in the local community who could help in times of trouble. This was not the case with Black people, as these clubs resisted integration for decades. Instead, Black people would use the church not just as a center for spiritual growth and practice but as a place to socialize and share a meal. In much the same way, Blacks were shut out of the political party process. If a Black person wanted to run for office, the parties often would not allow them to speak at the functions they held. To circumvent this problem, the Black churches allowed these politicians to use the church's pulpit as a way to drum up support for their campaign. The thought of a politician using the Sunday service as a means to politic seems completely inappropriate for most white Christians, but for the Black church, this was the only option that they had.

To further complicate matters, Black Protestants are theologically conservatives, sharing many of the same positions as their evangelical neighbors. Black Protestants are just as likely to believe that the Bible is literally true as evangelicals, and there is little difference in the two groups' views on same-sex marriage. Yet their politics are completely at odds. While vast swaths of evangelicals vote for Republicans, typically nine in ten Black Protestants vote for the Democratic candidate for president. The reasons for that are obviously complex, but much of the divergence can be found in the history of oppression that Black people have experienced in the United States. While evangelicals are often wary of the size and scope of the government, Black Protestants believe that the government has been one of the few institutions to support at all their voting rights and access to education.

Demographically, Black Protestants have seen a slow downward drift over the past three decades, which is displayed in figure 1.4. In the mid-1980s, almost one in ten Americans was affiliated with a Black Protestant tradition. That share has declined in the past twenty years. Now approximately 6 percent of Americans are Black Protestants. Why the decline? A big part of it is that while just 5 percent

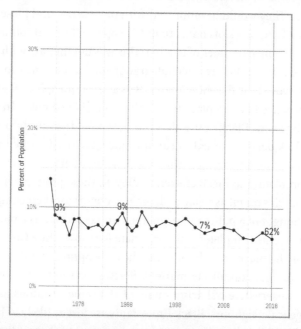

Figure 1.4. Black Protestants from 1972 to 2018.

Data from the General Social Survey, a project of the independent research organization NORC at the University of Chicago, with principal funding from the National Science Foundation, https://gss.norc.org/Get-The-Data.

of Black people said that they were religiously unaffiliated in 1980, that number has quadrupled in 2018 to 21 percent of the Black population—which, coincidentally, is almost the same trajectory as the rise of the nones in the entire American population. Coupled with the fact that the share of Americans who identify as African American has stayed stagnant over the past three decades, this will lead to an inevitable decline. In chapter 3, I will discuss how several demographics, including race, impact the rate of disaffiliation.

Catholics

The Catholic Church has always played a tremendous role in the religious landscape of the United States. Many eighteenth- and nineteenth-century immigrants came to this country from countries where the Catholic Church was the only choice for people seeking out a faith tradition. Many of the Irish fleeing from the potato famine landed in America wanting to build a new life but also retain the teachings and trappings of the Catholic Church. This was true for immigrants from the rest of Europe as well. Many of the largest cities in New England are overwhelmingly Catholic as a result of this great migration that occurred during the eighteenth and nineteenth centuries.

More recent immigrants to the United States have come from Central and South America, countries where the Catholic Church has been especially strong. However, this group of immigrants is more racially diverse. While the American Catholic Church had been overwhelmingly white for centuries, that is changing rapidly. In 2018, a quarter of all US Catholics were not white, and that share could grow exponentially in the coming decades as white birth rates slow compared to nonwhite Americans.

The Catholic Church is still one of the dominant religious institutions in the United States, but it seems to be in decline, especially in the past decade, which is apparent in figure 1.5. The Catholic share of the population was surprisingly stable from 1972 until the mid-2000s, when their portion of the population hovered between 25 and 27 percent. However, that number declined to 23 percent in 2018. While it would be unwise to pin this on any one cause, it's impossible

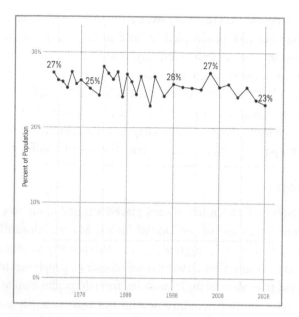

Figure 1.5. Catholics from 1972 to 2018.

Data from the General Social Survey, a project of the independent research organization NORC at the University of Chicago, with principal funding from the National Science Foundation, https://gss.norc.org/Get-The-Data.

to ignore the recent scandal involving cases of sexual abuse by priests. Many of these allegations began to receive media attention when the *Boston Globe* launched an investigation into them in the early 2000s. It's noteworthy that the share of Catholics who said that they attended Mass at least once a week was 45 percent in 1972, but just 20 percent in 2018. So, it would appear that the number of nonpracticing Catholics is growing, though the number of people who identify as Catholic has declined only slightly. American Catholics were statistically the same size as evangelicals and the religiously unaffiliated in 2018.

Jews

Judaism in the United States has had a long and complicated history. Many Jews arrived from Europe during great waves of migration in the 1800s. While Jewish synagogues can be found all over the

United States, they are typically concentrated in the Northeast, as many settlers put down roots in New England and the Rust Belt. American Jews have always been a numerically small portion of the population but have had an outsized role in American society and politics. Jewish Americans serve as an interesting puzzle for political scientists because they possess many of the traits that should lead to a Republican affiliation, such as earning solid family incomes and being almost completely Caucasian, but despite this, they are a strong Democratic voting bloc. The reasons for this are not entirely straightforward; however, one theory is that Jewish people see themselves as outsiders in their society and think the Democratic party has consistently tried to cater to marginalized population groups.[10]

It's crucial to remember just how small the Jewish population is in the United States, which is clear from figure 1.6. According to the

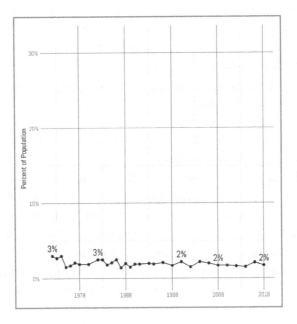

Figure 1.6. Jews from 1972 to 2018.

Data from the General Social Survey, a project of the independent research organization NORC at the University of Chicago, with principal funding from the National Science Foundation, https://gss.norc.org/Get-The-Data.

GSS, they made up 3 percent of Americans in 1972, and that number declined to 1.7 percent in 2018. To put that in perspective, that's about the same percentage as Buddhists and Hindus combined or about the same as Latter-day Saints. Because the decline has been so slight (just 1.3 percent over forty-six years), the size of the Jewish population was not statistically different in 2018 compared to 1972. However, Judaism is not just a religious affiliation but also a cultural identity, so many Jews who are not religiously active may still check the box for Jewish on surveys because of their ethnic ties to Judaism.

Observants of Other Faith Traditions

One of the primary difficulties in classifying religion in the United States is that once one moves away from the largest religious groups (mainly Protestants and Catholics), lots of small religious denominations must be classified. RELTRAD uses "other faith tradition" as a catchall for a variety of religious groups that are not large enough to justify their own category. Those who fall into this group come from a menagerie of backgrounds, including Muslims, Mormons, Buddhists, Hindus, pagans, and people who indicate that their religious affiliation is "other" on the GSS. Consequently, it's not possible to speak in broad terms about the contours of this politically, racially, and religiously diverse category.

What is notable, though, is that this group is consistently growing in size, which is visualized in figure 1.7. In the mid-1980s, just 3 percent of Americans were of another faith tradition, which was essentially the same size as the Jewish population. That share has risen slowly and steadily over the past several decades—reaching a peak of 6 percent in the latest wave of the GSS. There are several reasons for this increase. For instance, the Mormon church has grown about 1.5 percent per year in recent years.[11] But what is also fueling this increase is immigration to the United States. While a great many in the past came from regions of the world where Christianity was the dominant force, many recent arrivals to the United States have been from Asia. With them they bring a Buddhist, Hindu, or Muslim

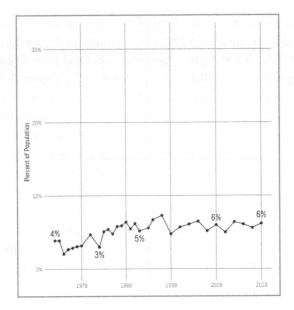

Figure 1.7. Other faith traditions from 1972 to 2018.

Data from the General Social Survey, a project of the independent research organization NORC at the University of Chicago, with principal funding from the National Science Foundation, https://gss.norc.org/Get-The-Data.

affiliation, which is also boosting these numbers. Additionally, more and more Americans are rejecting traditional labels like Protestant, Catholic, or Christian and are instead saying that they are merely spiritual, a choice that puts them in the "other faith tradition" category.

The Nones

Having surveyed the rest of the American religious landscape, we now turn to the subject of the inquiry—those who say that they have no religious affiliation. Consider this: of the six religious traditions that were detailed in this chapter, five are smaller today than they were in 1972. Just one—other faith traditions—is larger, and the increase there is just 2 percentage points. Between 2016 and 2018, those without religious ties rose 1.5 percentage points. The growth has not always been so exponential. For instance, from 1972 to 1990 the rate of increase was a total of 2 percentage points. However, something changed from 1991 to 1996 when the share of the nones jumped from 6 percent to 12 percent. To put it bluntly, 5 percent of the population disaffiliated in a five-year period. From that point forward, the nones have enjoyed what venture capitalists have called "hockey stick" growth, which is visualized in figure 1.8. With very few exceptions, the nones have grown consistently year on year since the mid-1990s, and it would appear that there is no end in sight.

Religious demography is a zero-sum game. If one religious tradition gets larger, then others have to get smaller. We can't add any water to this bathtub; we can only swirl it around. So where have the nones come from? The easy answer is mainline Protestant Christianity. As previously noted, mainline Protestants have declined from 30 percent of the population to just 10 percent in about four decades.

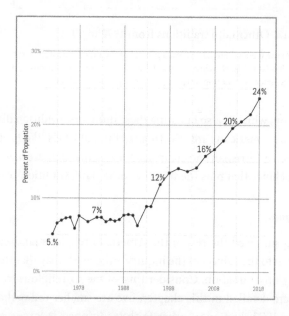

Figure 1.8. No religion from 1972 to 2018.

Data from the General Social Survey, a project of the independent research organization NORC at the University of Chicago, with principal funding from the National Science Foundation, https://gss.norc.org/Get-The-Data.

It would be convenient to claim that this explains the entirety of the rise of the nones, but that would be too simplistic. Consider the fact that evangelicals were 30 percent of Americans in 1993 but are now 22 percent. That eight-percentage-point drop has to affect another part of the bathtub as well. Couple this with the fact that Black Protestants, Catholics, and Jews have seen small declines as well, and we begin to see that the religiously unaffiliated have come from a variety of sources—not just moderate Protestants. I'll explore this phenomenon in greater depth later on.

HOW MANY NONES ARE THERE REALLY?

All these results from the GSS need to be understood in the context of the way other surveys ask about religious affiliation. The GSS's approach is to ask respondents, "What is your religious preference? Is it Protestant, Catholic, Jewish, some other religion, or no religion?" Most of those response options lead to follow-up questions about specific religious affiliation. For instance, if someone says that they are Protestant, then they are asked to specify their broad denominational family (Baptist, Methodist, etc.), and then are asked an additional question that tries to identify their specific tradition (e.g., United Methodist or Free Methodist). However, if someone chooses the "no religion" option, then that portion of the survey ends and they move on to a different topic. Note that the GSS does not ask if someone classifies themselves as an atheist or agnostic.

The approach that the Pew Research Center takes is entirely different. Instead of offering just five options up front like the GSS does, it has twelve different choices, ranging from the typical options of Protestant and Catholic to smaller groups like Mormons, Buddhists, and Muslims. In addition, the Pew approach offers a total of three options for people to select if they are religiously unaffiliated—atheist, agnostic, or a category simply titled "nothing in particular." So instead of just stating that an individual has "no religion," as in the GSS, the Pew approach delineates different types of religious "nones."

This approach has been adopted by the Cooperative Election Study (CES), which is based at Harvard University and has been done at least biannually since 2006. The CES is a wonderful resource for studying religion for three reasons. First, it is publicly available to anyone who wants to download the data and do some analysis. Second, it asks about religion in the same way the Pew Research Center does, which counts the aforementioned three types of religiously unaffiliated people. But most importantly, it has a huge sample size. While each wave of the GSS is around 2,500 people, the 2020 sample of the CES was 61,000. That means that even a population that makes up about 5 percent of all Americans (like atheists) still gives us a larger sample size than the entirety of the GSS sample. That allows a researcher to look at atheists by gender or race or any number of variables and still have a sample size with good statistical power.

However, this difference in methodology leaves researchers with a significant statistical discrepancy, which is clear from figure 1.9. In 2008, the CES reported that 24 percent of American adults had no religious affiliation: 4 percent were atheist, 5 percent were agnostic, and 15 percent were nothing in particular. That 2008 share is already higher than the GSS's estimate in 2018—ten years later—of 23 percent. And from there, the share of the nones in the CES continued to rise. By 2013, it hit 30 percent of the population, and by 2019 that figure eclipsed 35 percent. In the most recent data from 2021, 37 percent of all adults say that they have no religious affiliation. Note, however, that a majority of those nones are not atheists or agnostics (13 percent combined), but instead a group called "nothing in particular." We will take a deep dive into these three types of nones in chapter 4.

What is seemingly an easy question—how many nones are there?—is surprisingly difficult to answer. In figure 1.10, I compiled data from six different surveys: the previously included GSS and CES, plus statistics reported by the Pew Research Center, Gallup, the Democracy Fund's Nationscape survey, and data reported by the Public Religion Research Institute (PRRI). When looking at the long-term trend lines, the numbers for the GSS, Pew, and PRRI are

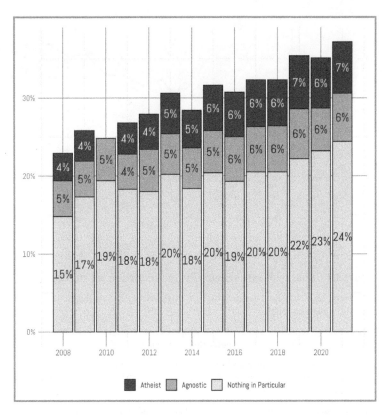

Figure 1.9. The rise of the nones, 2008 to 2021.

Data from Stephen Ansolabehere, Brian F. Schaffner, and Sam Luks, Cooperative Congressional Election Study, Cambridge, MA: Harvard University, http://cces.gov. harvard.edu.

largely in sync for most of the last decade. However, there are some deviations. For instance, PRRI reports that the share of Americans who are nones declined between 2018 and 2020 by about two percentage points. That's not replicated in other datasets. Additionally, the most recent estimates of the nones varies widely. It's clear that the CES reports the largest share of nones at 37 percent in 2021. Pew Research Center, the General Social Survey, and the Nationscape survey put the nones at 29 percent, 28 percent, and 26 percent respectively. PRRI reports the nones much lower at 23

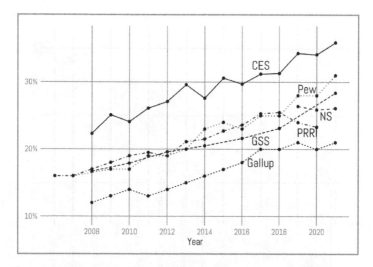

Figure 1.10. Share who are religiously unaffiliated in six surveys.

Data from Public Religion Research Institute. https://www.prri.org/research/2020-census-of-american-religion/

Data from Pew Research Center. https://www.pewresearch.org/religion/2021/12/14/about-three-in-ten-u-s-adults-are-now-religiously-unaffiliated/

Data from Tausanovitch, Chris and Lynn Vavreck. 2021. Democracy Fund + UCLA Nationscape Project, October 10-17, 2019 (version 20211215). https://www.voterstudygroup.org/nationscape

Data from Stephen Ansolabehere, Brian F. Schaffner, and Sam Luks, Cooperative Congressional Election Study, Cambridge, MA: Harvard University, http://cces.gov.harvard.edu.

Data from the General Social Survey, a project of the independent research organization NORC at the University of Chicago, with principal funding from the National Science Foundation, https://gss.norc.org/Get-The-Data

Data from Gallup. https://news.gallup.com/poll/1690/religion.aspx

percent in 2020, while Gallup puts the share at 21 percent in 2021. The Gallup numbers represent the lowest estimate, and that's more than likely due to the fact they still use phone calls to collect their sample, a topic that will be addressed below. Finally, because the Nationscape survey was only conducted during an eighteen-month window of time, it represents a snapshot of American religion in 2019 and 2020 instead of a longitudinal trend. When I am asked in an interview what percentage of Americans have no religious affiliation, I think the most statistically sound answer is "about 30 percent."

So what's going on here? How can we explain these wide discrepancies among different surveys? It's impossible to know exactly which estimate is most accurate. A good portion of survey research is trying to get inside the mind of the person who is taking the survey. One possible reason for the divergence is that some surveys give people more options. For instance, the addition of the "nothing in particular" category seems to be giving permission to people who are very marginally attached to religion to go ahead and select that option. Maybe it appears to be less judgmental than the "no religion" option in the GSS. There's also the issue of survey administration. Some of these surveys used to be conducted face to face, as in the case of the GSS, while some are administered completely online through a web browser. Just the mode of delivery can have a tremendous impact on how people answer questions, an idea that we will explore in more detail in chapter 2.

I have looked at religion data for over fifteen years, and I am left with the impression that giving people more ways to declare their religious preference likely results in more accurate results. Therefore, moving forward, I will typically be using the classification scheme put forth by Pew (and replicated in the CES) to describe the religiously unaffiliated as three distinct groups—atheists, agnostics, and those who believe in nothing in particular. Because the GSS only gives one overarching category—those of no religion—it's impossible to make distinctions among the different types of "nones." One of the primary goals of this work is to illustrate, in some detail, that nones are not created equal. Lumping atheists together with those who say that they are "nothing in particular" is both theoretically and practically inappropriate, as the two groups think, act, and vote in completely different ways.

To summarize, American religion is both incredibly volatile in some segments and also highly consistent in others. While most traditions have seen small shifts in size over the past four decades, two groups have changed rapidly—mainline Protestants and the religiously unaffiliated. On average it seems that many people who would have identified as mainline thirty years ago now say they have no religious connection. In essence, moderate Protestants are going extinct, while conservative Christianity is holding the line. In 2018, the GSS indicated that the "nones" were now the same size statistically as Roman Catholics and evangelical Protestants, with simple projections suggesting that the nones will likely be the largest religious group in America inside a decade. Despite the fact that three in ten American adults are religiously unaffiliated, scholarship on this growing religious segment has lagged far behind work that tries to explain the social and political worlds of other religious groups, like evangelicals and Catholics.

I've spent quite a bit of time explaining what has happened to American religion over the past four decades. However, I have not yet tried to answer an even more difficult question: Why is it happening? More specifically, Why are the nones on a path to being the largest religious group in America in the next decade? As is often the case in the social science world, the answer is "It's complicated." It's crucial to remind ourselves that nearly 30 percent of Americans didn't decide to move away from religion at the same time or for the same reason. Everyone who became a none got there by their own path. While I can try to illuminate some of the broadest and most well-trod avenues for this shift, it's impossible to understand all the side roads and back alleys that some people have taken as they've moved away from religion. However, a more robust view of the cultural, political, and demographic changes in the United States over the past four decades can hopefully shed some light on this area.

CHAPTER 2

A Social Scientist
Tries to Explain
Religious Disaffiliation

"So why is all this happening?"

It's a question that haunts my dreams, to be honest. In every interview I do about American religion, eventually it will all come back to that question. A lot of the time, I'm scheduled for an eight-minute radio spot and know that to answer that query with any measure of scientific precision, I would need at least an hour. So I give the kind of very abbreviated and overly reductive answer that I'm sure makes a lot of my academic colleagues cringe, leaving out a lot of the nuance that exists in the social world and completely ignoring well-established work by many of my friends. I feel terrible about doing that, but that's the nature of talking to the media.

The truth is, I can't point to one single causal mechanism for the nones's astronomically growing numbers, and no other academic can either. The problem with social science is that it's the study of people. People are emotional, unpredictable, and completely unintelligible most of the time. When I teach a course in American voting behavior, I impress upon my students that tens of thousands of pages are written every year trying to understand what goes through a person's mind when they cast a ballot on election day. They might be reflecting on months of thorough research and careful consideration of the future of American monetary policy. Or it could be that they didn't like one candidate's haircut.

The same challenges arise when studying American religion. One individual can leave a church after years of spiritual soul-searching because they have a sophisticated theological disagreement with the pastor about transubstantiation. Others leave because the congregation moved the Sunday service half an hour. Broad strokes are the name of the game for all social scientists. Those of us who study American religion are not in the business of understanding why a specific individual left or changed religious affiliation; instead, we are trying to understand, at a broad level, what factors lead most people to leave church behind. Some of you will surely read the following pages and think, "I didn't leave church for *any* of those reasons." And you're right. Each individual who walks away from religion has their own reasons and their own spiritual journey. Social science can't get too hung up on explaining the outliers; rather, we have to strive to understand what happened to the average person.

I am reminded of my first graduate course in research methodology. The topic of discussion was the eminent sociologist Emile Durkheim's book *Suicide*. His research question was a simple one: What are the factors that lead someone to take their own life? To conduct that study, Durkheim went to morgues around Paris and collected the death certificates of those who had committed suicide. Using very basic statistics, Durkheim elucidated the factors that made suicide more or less likely. As we were discussing Durkheim's work amongst ourselves, one student said, "I think that Durkheim's work is a bit offensive, because he doesn't seem to care much about the individual lives lost to suicide." Our professor, Dr. Scott McClurg, responded by saying, "As a social scientist, I am much less interested in why John Smith committed suicide, than why people like John Smith take their own life." In short, each person matters to social science. But, I am more concerned with how those individual stories aggregate to larger patterns in social and cultural change. It's just the nature of social science inquiry.

As we move into the next section, I would caution you to think carefully about some of the larger unseen forces in American society that may make the decision to change religious affiliation easier or more difficult. Those invisible factors can be cultural, political, theological, or just the spirit of the times. And as a pastor, I never want to discount the work of the Holy Spirit in people's lives which can push them in a variety of spiritual directions. If you have left a faith tradition behind, think carefully about when and why that happened. There may be factors that influenced your decision that only make sense in hindsight. With all those caveats laid out, let's turn to some of the major theories that explain the rise of the nones.

SECULARIZATION

One of the oldest theories in the sociology of religion is called secularization. This theory contends that as a society gains higher levels of educational achievement and economic prosperity, the result will be a gradual move away from religion. This theory was written about extensively by some of the most influential and foundational social scientists, including Durkheim, Karl Marx, and Max Weber. The overarching implication of secularization theory is that eventually all countries on Earth will reach a point where religion is either largely marginalized or completely nonexistent.

To give some historical context for this view of modern society, it's crucial to understand how some anthropologists think about the role religion played in ancient societies. For almost the entirety of recorded human history, civilizations have been formed around and endured because of their ability to feed their citizens. Feeding oneself used to require living a nomadic lifestyle, following livestock around as they grazed the countryside. At some point (which is fiercely debated among academics), human beings began to grow crops in an organized fashion, giving way to an agrarian society.[1] The ability of individuals to reap a bountiful harvest was an essential component of the growth and advancement of human civilization.

If the survival of an entire species is predicated on their ability to raise enough crops, it's no surprise that humans became obsessed with the weather. Too much rain, a prolonged drought, inadequate sunshine, or an insect infestation could lead to not just a disastrous harvest but also a large percentage of your town nearly starving to death until the next growing season. In an attempt to stave off such a calamity, civilizations began to look for explanations for droughts, pestilence, and other natural disasters. Naturally, many of those explanations related to the divine. If the rain came at the proper time, that was God rewarding good behavior, but if some disaster befell the community, that must be evidence of wrongdoing in their midst.[2]

German sociologist Max Weber argued that as rationality and scientific discovery began to explode after the Enlightenment, human beings began to see the error of their ways and came to understand rain as the outcome of scientific processes, not the result of divine intervention. The German word Weber used to describe this shift in understanding, *Entzauberung*, is often translated "disenchantment" in English, but the literal translation seems much more fitting: "de-magic-ation." Thus Weber argues that civilizations used to understand their world through superstition but now have the tools of science and rationality to guide their activities.[3]

The founder of communist theory, Karl Marx, believed that religion was an artificial structure created by those in power as a means to keep the underclass subservient to the whims of the bourgeoisie. Marx famously wrote, "[Religion] is the opium of the people."[4] For Marx, religion was a tool of oppression used by those with power and a way for people with less power to psychologically cope with the poor treatment they were receiving as they worked in factories full time. Thus the goal for Marx was to get people to realize that they were being subjected to violence by the rich and well-connected elites. Marx believed it was his duty to help promote class consciousness—to make the working class aware of how they were being exploited by the ruling class. The famous last words of *The Communist Manifesto* make this plain: "Workers of all countries, unite!" For Marx, class consciousness was elusive but inevitable, and when it was achieved, religion would lose its utility and recede from society.

The primary evidence that supports secularization is seen in Europe and is visualized in figure 2.1. In many countries on the European continent where dozens of religious wars have been fought over the past several hundred years, very few people actually attend church with any regularity. I calculated the share of people in twenty-nine European countries who attended church once a week or more in 2018 and 2020. Notice that Poland and Slovakia have high levels of religious attendance—and that those are clearly outliers. In Italy, the center of Catholicism, religious adherence matches that of the United States, with just one in four attending services once a week.

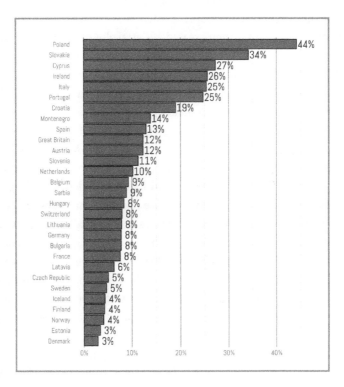

Figure 2.1. Percent attending church weekly.

Data from the European Social Survey, https://www.europeansocialsurvey.org/.

Other populous European countries like Spain and Great Britain have attendance rates in the low teens, while in Germany and France, fewer than one in ten of their citizens attend church once a week or more. While there are no reliable measures of European religiosity before the 1970s, the hundreds of vacant churches that exist across the continent bear witness to the reality that Europe has become an overwhelmingly secular continent since World War II.[5]

Yet despite all the evidence that developed democracies have cast off religion as they have gained higher levels of educational and economic advancement, one case is clearly an outlier from this trend—the United States. To visualize that, I grabbed some World Bank data related to the gross domestic product (GDP) per capita from ninety-six countries, as well as data from the Pew Research Center about the percentage of people in each country who said religion was very important. I then created a scatterplot of the relationship between those two variables, which is displayed in figure 2.2.

Notice that the trend line is high on the left side of the graph and low on the right side, which indicates a clear negative relationship between GDP and the importance of religion. Said another way, as a country becomes more economically prosperous, it is less religious. This confirms the theories laid out by Weber and Marx. However, there are some major outliers on the graph. In the bottom left, we see countries like China, Russia, and Estonia, which according to the linear model should be much more religious than they are currently, based on economic output. We can easily chalk that up to the communist governments that went out of their way to discourage religious belief in the past seventy-five years.[6] However, the other outlier is on the right side of the graph—the United States. According to this simple model, the share of American citizens in the United States who should rate religion as very important is approaching zero based on the country's economic prosperity.

There are several explanations for why secularization theory doesn't work in the case of the United States. One argues that the United States is an exceptional country, so the social science theories about religion and economic advancement just don't apply. Some

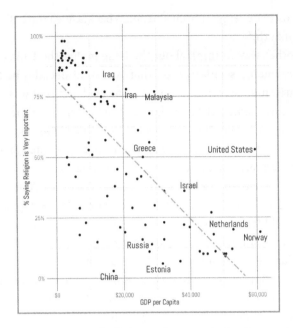

Figure 2.2. Importance of religion and economic development.

Data from World Bank, "GDP per Capita (Current US$)," https://tinyurl.com/y967okgt; and Pew Research Center, "The Global Religious Landscape," December 18, 2012, https://tinyurl.com/y6gqdfl4.

have argued that American society is a decidedly individualistic one where authority is distrusted, and the low-church ethos of many Protestant churches appeals to the antiestablishment predispositions of many Americans.[7] Another explanation comes from the French social scientist Alexis de Tocqueville who visited the United States just a few years after its founding and was surprised by the strong separation of church and state. As de Tocqueville put it, "Religion cannot share the material might of those who govern without incurring some of the hatred they inspire."[8] In essence, American religion dodged a bullet by not being sponsored by the state. Finally, some social scientists credit the religious pluralism of the United States as the cause of American exceptionalism. The fact that no one tradition encompasses more than 30 percent of the American population might insulate religion from a national backlash against all expressions of faith.[9]

Another way to think about the issue is that the United States is experiencing secularization that is several decades behind in comparison to countries in Europe. The evidence that was laid out in the prior chapter related to the astronomical rise in the religiously unaffiliated does provide tacit evidence that the United States is seeing a wave of delayed secularization and that the United States will likely look more and more like Europe as time passes.

There have been scholars who have questioned whether secularization is an "iron law" of social science. For instance, Pippa Norris and Ronald Inglehart believe that the prosperity of a country is less important than the educational and economic advancement of the individual citizen. For these scholars, human beings are on a search for existential security—that is, a desire to reduce uncertainty to a manageable level. People want to ensure that if they fall ill, they will have access to adequate care, or if their house burns down, they can quickly and easily find a place to stay. However, even in prosperous countries like the United States, those at the lower end of the socio-economic spectrum have less insulation against tragedy, and therefore a belief in God becomes a coping mechanism to quell the uncertainty of misfortune. Income inequality would obviously exacerbate this religious divide. In the United States, where income inequality is noticeably larger than Western Europe, the theory would predict higher levels of religiosity for those at the bottom of the income spectrum. For Inglehart and Norris, a search for comfort explains why the United States saw a huge resurgence in professed faith in the aftermath of 9/11—because Americans from all backgrounds experienced a significant decline in their feeling of security and therefore tried to compensate by returning to faith.[10]

There's also been some recent work that points to the conclusion that secularization theory may have borne out in the case of the Western world but may not be replicated as other parts of the world see rapid economic advancement due to globalization. In a quantitative analysis of a hundred countries over three decades, Kodai

Kusano and Waleed Ahmad Jami found that while western European countries like Spain, France, and Germany tended to become less religious as they modernized, that wasn't the case in post-communist parts of the world. Their work finds that in countries like China, Bulgaria, and Russia, religiosity has accelerated quite dramatically over the last thirty years. Part of this rise may be because some individuals were more comfortable expressing their true religious beliefs once Communist governments were no longer in power. But the authors have an alternate theory—that this rise in religiosity relates back to Norris and Inglehart's claim about existential security. When many countries emerged out of communism and grew rapidly, economic inequality accelerated, leaving the majority of citizens worried about their ability to feed their families or find adequate healthcare. Rising insecurity led to increased levels of religiosity. By this argument, modernization leading to secularization is not a foregone conclusion for all parts of the world.[11]

SOCIAL DESIRABILITY BIAS

One of the great things about academia is that we create fancy terms for things that are very simple. "Social desirability bias" is a nice way of saying that people lie. More specifically, it refers to the well-documented phenomenon that people don't tell the truth when asked survey questions because they want to look good in the eyes of the person conducting the survey. When I describe this concept to people, often a few chuckles erupt around the room—an understandable reaction. However, for social scientists, this is an especially pernicious problem that weakens our ability to be certain about the results we collect when we put a survey into the field.

What do people lie about on surveys? Controversial areas of American social life are the usual suspects. For instance, if you were asked by a female survey administrator whether women are less qualified than men to become president of the United States, would you answer yes if that was your honest answer? Or if a Black person asked if you think Black people are lazier than white people and you did hold that belief, would you say what you really think? Of course, lots of people are going to mask their true feelings while being questioned by a survey collector. But racism and sexism are not the only areas in which people consistently misreport their true feelings. Social scientists who study things like sexual behavior struggle to get a true measurement of how much pornography people watch, how frequently they masturbate, or whether they have ever had an affair. Those who study drug use also know that most people underreport their actual behavior. We know that many people will not admit that they have smoked marijuana, and it's very likely that they will significantly downplay how much alcohol they consume as well.

However, ground zero for social desirability bias may be religious activity. Despite the fact that more and more Americans are indicating that they are religiously unaffiliated, US culture still holds to a sense of a civil religion—the assumption that Americans should believe in God and attend church.[12] For instance, Pew has published survey research indicating that the majority of Americans believe religion does more good than harm, strengthens society, and brings people together.[13] This sense that being involved in church is a positive social behavior provides clear evidence that any survey that asks religious questions is going to be shot through with social desirability bias.

One of my favorite examples of this problem is the case of Ashtabula County in northeastern Ohio. A team of researchers conducted a telephone poll of adults in the county to ask a series of questions about respondents' religious activity, including church attendance. Overall, 35.8 percent of Protestants said that they attended church weekly. After the survey had been administered, the research team created a database of every Protestant church in the county using telephone books, property records, and newspaper advertisements. Having organized this list, the researchers then sent a letter to each church asking them to report their average attendance over the past year. If churches didn't respond, surveyors counted cars in the parking lots and used both collection methods to generate an estimate of overall attendance. The researchers concluded that the average percentage of Protestants who attended church in Ashtabula County was just 19.6. In essence, half of the people who said they attend church once a week lied about it.[14]

The affect of social desirability bias on the ability of researchers to obtain a full and accurate count of the religiously unaffiliated cannot be overstated. The clearest implication is that lots of people are actually not religious at all, but they are afraid to say as much to a survey researcher. In effect, there are many more nones than surveys indicate. But trying to pinpoint the pervasiveness of social desirability bias is nearly impossible. To illustrate just how difficult it is to isolate, I calculated two things: the share of Americans who say that they have no religious affiliation as well as the percentage of Protestants and Catholics who say they never attend religious services. The results are displayed in figure 2.3.

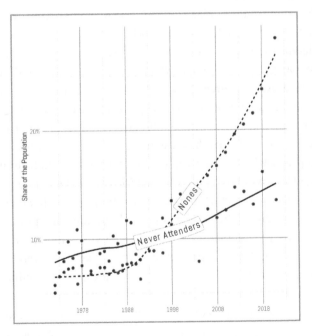

Figure 2.3. Looking for evidence of social desirability bias.

Data from the General Social Survey, a project of the independent research organization NORC at the University of Chicago, with principal funding from the National Science Foundation, https://gss.norc.org/Get-The-Data.

Part of being a social scientist is trying to make educated guesses about how respondents will reveal their preferences in a survey without explicitly asking them for their real opinions. In this case, it seems possible people would be more likely to admit that they are a "never-attending" Protestant or Catholic than to just say the truth: they have no religious affiliation. What the data should indicate, then, is that the share of Christians who say that they never attend church has declined as the percentage of the religiously unaffiliated has risen. However, that's not what the data indicates. In fact, somewhat surprisingly, the share of the religiously unaffiliated has skyrocketed (as previously described), but at the same time, the percentage of people who say they are Christians but also say they never attend services is also up (from about 10 percent in 1993 to 15 percent in 2021).

Social desirability bias could still be having an affect here but possibly in a more subtle way. Consider this explanation of religious affiliation. In reality, there is a continuum from affiliation to disaffiliation. On one end are people who report both a religious affiliation and some level of church attendance. On the other end are those who say that they are not attached to religion, nor do they attend church. In the middle are those who are affiliated or indicate religious attendance. It's possible that the erosion of social desirability bias has led some people who were never-attending affiliates to disaffiliate and has also led to some marginally attached Christians (like those who say they attend once a year) to now say that they never attend religious services. In effect, the erosion of social desirability bias pushes large portions of the population to report their actual religious affiliation and behavior. A logical prediction is that as social desirability bias becomes less noticeable, then even more of the never-attending affiliates will become nones.

That's not to say that social science has not tried to find ways around social desirability bias. For instance, some public opinion researchers have begun using a list experiment in their surveys. The way this works is that the sample is split into two groups. The first group is given three statements that are typically benign in their content. They are asked to tell the survey administrator how many of the statements they agree with instead of agreeing or disagreeing to each one. The other half of the sample is given the same three neutral statements, plus a more controversial one, and then asked how many they agree with from the list. If the first group, on average, agreed with 2.5 statements, while the second group agreed with 3 statements on average, we can reasonably assume that 50 percent of Americans agreed with the controversial statement that was included in the second survey group. The logic behind this is straightforward: the group that gets the three benign statements helps us arrive at the baseline number of agreement. In this case, we can assume that if several hundred people were given those same statements, the average level of agreement would be 2.5. If the group that gets the three neutral statements plus the controversial one has an average agreement of three, then we can reasonably assume that what raised the average from 2.5 to 3 is that half of the sample agreed with that fourth controversial statement. This type of experimental survey design has been used to study views of religion by social scientists. For instance, work by Benjamin Knoll and Cammie Jo Bolin found that when using a list experiment, over half of survey respondents supported female clergy, which was lower than the share who agreed with female pastors when asked the question more directly. This indicates that social desirability bias led some respondents to indicate that they were supportive of women religious leaders when they were not.[15]

The most frustrating thing about social desirability bias is that current researchers are completely powerless to assess its pervasiveness in surveys conducted decades ago. Even if we could get a list of all those who responded to the General Social Survey (GSS) in 1988 and found a way to contact them, how would we ask the question, "Were you lying about going to church when asked thirty years ago?" And if they said that they were being truthful about their religiosity in the late 1980s, how would we know that they aren't lying now? It's the Gordian Knot of public opinion research, and while many of us know that it always hangs over estimates of religious behavior in decades past, we know that we will never be able to derive a more accurate estimate from previously collected data. But, as previously mentioned, there's ample reason to believe that social desirability is declining because the stigma against nonreligious Americans is significantly less pervasive today than it was a few decades ago.

From a social science standpoint, this is unquestionably a good thing. If social desirability bias is actually waning—and the evidence seems to indicate that it is—academics are increasingly able to accurately identify the religiously unaffiliated in their survey samples. That leads to a more accurate portrait of American social life. But what does this mean for those who do the hard work of preparing to preach and lead worship every Sunday? How should pastors feel about the fact that about 30 percent of Americans are unaffiliated and an increasing number of Catholics and Protestants say they never attend services? It's easy to look at those skyward-pointing trend lines and get discouraged, but it's possible, and probably even likely, that many millions of people were just not being honest with the survey administrators decades ago. Now we are seeing an accurate picture of American religion. Not to be overly cliché, but the first step in recovery is recognizing you have a problem. Maybe an individual who is willing to be honest about where they stand in matters of spirituality is more open to reconsidering their future than someone who is not being honest with themselves.

THE INTERNET

Social desirability bias is important because social science needs to find a way to explain why it has become more socially acceptable in recent years for people to be religiously unaffiliated or to report their actual level of church attendance to a survey administrator. Obviously, it's not a good idea to ask people taking a survey, "Are you going to lie to us when you answer these questions?" Yet there are always forces in society that make telling the truth a little bit easier or more difficult. One primary development may explain a great deal of this shift toward more honesty in American society surrounding religion: the internet.

Imagine if someone was born in 1960 in rural Mississippi, a place that is overwhelmingly politically conservative and also nearly unanimously Christian. If that individual, for whatever reason, began to doubt the existence of God and eventually viewed themselves as an atheist, would they want to make that belief known to their friends and family? It's highly likely that this individual would go their entire life never meeting a fellow Mississippian who shared the same beliefs about God. The academic community has a term for this experience: *the spiral of silence.*

The German political scientist Elisabeth Noelle-Neumann described the spiral of silence in the late 1970s. Noelle-Neumann believed that every individual has an inherent desire to blend into a group and to avoid social isolation at all costs. Therefore, people are attuned to what opinions are being espoused with confidence in the public square. If an individual's view of the world is in line with the one they hear being discussed, they will join in boldly. However, if one perceives that their opinion is not held in high regard by their community, then they will become willfully silent. People naturally assume that silence is agreement, and therefore, the people who hold the majority opinion will become louder and more forceful, while those who initially stayed silent will have even less incentive to voice their disagreement as time passes.[16]

There is some scientific evidence to support a belief that the spiral of silence theory may not function the same way on the internet. In fact, some studies have shown that minority opinion holders are even more apt to speak up in an anonymous online environment.[17] However, on social media, where users are more often identified by their real names and share photos and other personal information, the spiral of silence still persists, just as it does in the face-to-face.[18] But the internet does seem like an ideal space for someone who is struggling with religious belief to find a community that will either help them work through their doubts or give them permission to walk away from their faith entirely. For instance, Reddit, an anonymous social media platform, has a number of forums that could reinforce users' belief systems. Parts of the site entitled "Debate a Christian" or "Debate an Atheist" have tens of thousands of subscribers, and a subreddit entitled "Atheism" has 2.7 million members. In comparison, the "Christianity" subreddit has just 325,000 subscribers. Clearly, if the aforementioned hypothetical Mississippi atheist was born in 1990 instead of 1960, they would be much more likely to find compatriots in the digital realm.

But does the rise in the share of internet users directly translate to the explosive growth of the nones? The data just doesn't tell a clear story. I visualized the share of Americans who owned a personal computer as well as those who had internet at home and then compared that to the rise of the religiously unaffiliated for figure 2.4. First, it's

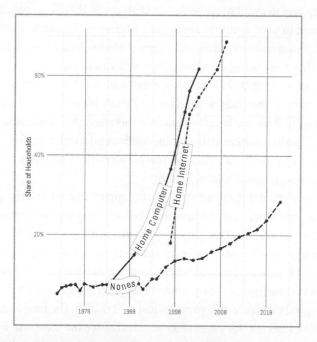

Figure 2.4. The rise in technology and the rise of the nones.

Data from the United States Census Bureau, "Computer and Internet Use in the United States: 1984 to 2009," February 2010, https://tinyurl.com/yyv54yv7.

important to note just how quickly home internet became common in the United States. While just 18 percent had a connection in 1997, that share jumped to 41.5 percent in just three years; the total number of households who had internet access in their homes tripled in just six years. Yet the religiously unaffiliated rose from 7 percent to 13 percent from 1990 to 1998, when just small shares of Americans had access to that technology.

It is likely that many millions of Americans now declare they are religiously unaffiliated because of things that they have seen or read on the internet. It's very possible that without its widespread adoption, the trend line for the nones would be much flatter. However, the problem for social science is that as the internet changed, so did a lot of other parts of American society. It would be irresponsible not to mention that the internet has likely also had a polarizing impact on other parts of American life as well, especially politics. It's possible that this polarization has galvanized Americans so many people feel they have to pick sides—Republicans versus Democrats, believing in something versus having no religious affiliation.

POLITICS

Maybe I am slightly biased because I am a trained political scientist, but I have always felt that the best and clearest explanation for the rapid rate of religious disaffiliation can be traced back to the recent political history of the United States. In recent years, everyone who studies religion and politics has been constantly confronted with the same statistic: 81 percent of white evangelicals voted for Donald Trump in the 2016 and 2020 presidential elections.[19] While many political observers were quick to note that the GOP and white evangelicals have consistently had a strong relationship, many pundits viewed the 81 percent figure as some sort of statistical aberration when in reality it was just business as usual. In fact, in 2008, 79 percent of white evangelicals voted for John McCain for president, and 77 percent of them cast a ballot for Mitt Romney in 2012.[20] Outside of

Black Protestants, there is no more politically homogeneous religious group than white evangelical Protestants.

It's important to understand that the connection between the devoutly religious and the Republican Party hasn't always been this strong. In fact, in 1978, half of all white weekly churchgoers identified as Democrats, while today just one quarter do.[21] This shift to the right side of the political spectrum among the devoutly religious may have ignited a backlash whereby political moderates and liberals fled church in droves when their political beliefs were challenged.

So how did this happen? How did white Christianity (especially white evangelicalism) become synonymous with conservative politics? The answer is one that is hotly debated among religious historians. Perhaps the most widely cited theory is that a group of conservative evangelical pastors who had gained a great deal of notoriety by becoming televangelists began to use their media platform to speak of the ills of American society. Discussion centered around issues like homosexuality, pornography, and abortion. Using these issues as flashpoints, they organized what became known as the religious right, which sparked widespread protests against the Equal Rights Amendment, homosexuality, and abortion.[22]

However, other scholars have questioned whether these culture war issues were really the impetus for such a potent political movement. Dartmouth professor Randall Balmer has detailed a counter-narrative about the religious right that focuses not on morality but instead on racism. More specifically, Balmer argues that the most important Supreme Court case for the religious right was not *Roe v. Wade* in 1973 but one that was decided two years earlier: *Green v. Connally*. It concerned Holmes County, Mississippi, which had chartered three private Christian schools in the wake of public-school desegregation. As a result, not a single white student attended a public school in Holmes County by the mid-1960s. The IRS denied the three schools a tax-exempt status, and the schools sued, losing at the Supreme Court. Following this, Bob Jones University, a fundamentalist school that did not admit Black students, also had its tax-exempt status revoked. Many in the religious right found this to be an encroachment on religious freedom, using it as a rallying cry to whip up more support for their cause of racial segregation.[23]

One final explanation comes from the Princeton historian Kevin Kruse, who believes that the true genesis of the movement lies not in morality or racism but instead in economics. Kruse contends that a group of wealthy, well-connected businessmen were growing tired of the high levels of taxation and regulation imposed upon them by Roosevelt's New Deal programs. If they tried to fight these regulations directly, they would look self-interested and greedy. Instead, they began to encourage and mobilize pastors all over the country to decry the evils of socialism and extol the virtues of free-market capitalism. It was this movement that led to the addition of "under God" to the Pledge of Allegiance and the printing of "In God We Trust" on our currency. In essence, these were efforts to inoculate the American public against the encroachment of atheistic communism.[24]

It's possible that all three of these—morality, racism, and economics—have played a role in the fusion that exists between white American religion and political conservatism in the twenty-first century. No matter what the cause, the melding of these two groups is almost complete. For instance, in 2018, 93 percent of all white Protestants attended a church in which Donald Trump's approval rating was above the national average of 40 percent. Additionally, sixteen of the twenty largest Protestant denominations moved toward the right end of the political spectrum between 2008 and 2018.[25] In essence, devout Protestant Christians are Republicans, with very few exceptions.

The belief that politics was having an unmistakable impact on the American religious landscape emerged in scholarly literature as early as 2002, when Michael Hout and Claude Fischer published a paper titled "Why More Americans Have No Religious Preference: Politics and Generations," in which they began to explicate, using statistical data, the fact that disaffiliation was occurring almost entirely among people who placed themselves on the left side of the political spectrum. To illustrate that, they broke the General Social Survey (GSS) up into five different ideological groups—liberals, those who lean liberal, moderates, those who lean conservative,

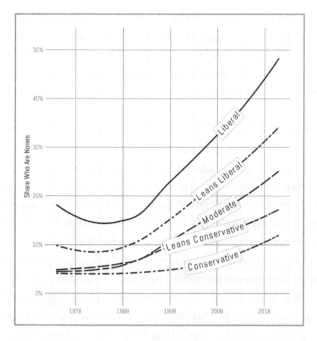

Figure 2.5. Political explanations for religious disaffiliation.

Data from the General Social Survey, a project of the independent research organization NORC at the University of Chicago, with principal funding from the National Science Foundation, https://gss.norc.org/Get-The-Data.

and conservatives—and then calculated the share of each group that reported that they had no religious affiliation for each year in the GSS.[26] Their data ends in 2002, but I have replicated and extended their analysis in figure 2.5.

What can be observed is clear and unmistakable—disaffiliation is directly related to political ideology. In fact, there's no deviation in the pattern as one moves from the left side of the ideological spectrum to the right: the rate of disaffiliation drops significantly. To put some numbers from 2021 on it, the unaffiliated included 51 percent of liberals, 36 percent of those who lean liberal, 27 percent of moderates, 20 percent of those who lean conservative, and just 12 percent of those who identified as conservative. A liberal is nearly twice as likely as a moderate and almost five times more likely than a political conservative to be unaffiliated. It's crucial to consider that it's not always been like this. For instance, in 1988, 15 percent of liberals were unaffiliated, but for the remaining four categories, the range was between 5 and 9 percent, and the differences weren't statistically significant. It's fair to say that liberals have always been more likely to be unaffiliated, but the disparity has never been so large.

There is a strong counterargument to be made on this point, though. One of the most difficult problems that researchers face in studying religion and politics is endogeneity—the idea that we can never be sure which way the causal arrow goes. To put it more simply, we cannot answer this question: Do our politics impact our religious affiliation, or does our religiosity have an impact on what political party we identify with? Recent scholarship seems to be pointing more and more to an understanding of politics as the first cause and religious affiliation lying downstream from that. Instead of deciding who they will cast a ballot for based on their religious tradition, most Americans pick a church that lines up with their view of the political world. For instance, Michele Margolis used data that tracked high-school seniors who graduated in 1965 as they moved through the next three decades of their lives. What she found was that when this cohort was in their twenties, Democrats and Republicans displayed no significant difference in their church attendance. But when those study subjects moved into their thirties, a clear partisan difference emerged—Republicans were still attending church at high rates, while Democrats reported a significant drop in religious attendance. As these subjects were surveyed into the earlier 2000s, the pew gap only widened. The connection between political conservativism and religiosity has kept many Republicans in the pews, while it's pushed scores of Democrats away from religion entirely. A stunning reality is coming into sharper focus: political concerns are driving religious behavior more than theological beliefs are guiding political principles.[27] Other surveys that were conducted during the run-up to the 2016 presidential election found that 14 percent of people left their house of worship in the immediate aftermath of Donald Trump's victory over Hillary Clinton. Those reporting a significant drop in church attendance were predominantly moderates and liberals who felt like their churches were more conservative than they were, and thus they made their way to the exits. In short, politics is driving religiosity much more than a religious worldview is shaping political opinions.[28]

There's little hope of this partisan divide being overcome in the near future. In fact, the data is pointing toward just the opposite. Over the last decade, the Cooperative Election Study has asked respondents to place themselves in ideological space on a scale from 1 (very liberal) to 7 (very conservative), with four denoting a "middle of the road" position. Atheists and agnostics view the Republican party as becoming more conservative as time passes—moving a half point to the right between 2014 and 2019, as can be seen in figure 2.6. At the same time, atheists and agnostics see themselves as becoming more

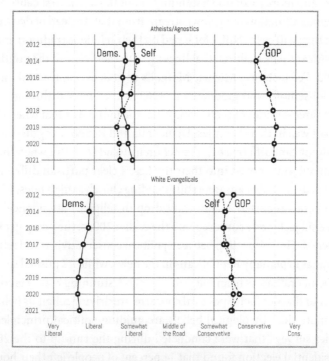

Figure 2.6. Place yourself, Democrats, and Republicans in ideological space.

Data from Stephen Ansolabehere, Brian F. Schaffner, and Sam Luks, Cooperative Congressional Election Study, Cambridge, MA: Harvard University, http://cces.gov.harvard.edu.

liberal over time. White evangelicals perceive that the Democrats have become more extreme while they themselves have drifted slowly to the right. It's almost like these two groups have a completely different perception of the American political landscape. White evangelicals put the Democrats at 1.5 on a 7-point scale in 2021, while atheists and agnostics see the Democrats closer to a 3. While atheists and agnostics see the GOP at 6.5, white evangelicals place them at 5.5 in 2021.

The data points from both figure 2.5 and figure 2.6 paint an alarming portrait of American religious and political life. First, the connection between identifying as a political liberal and having no religious affiliation has grown over time, while political conservatives are still overwhelmingly people of faith. At the same time, atheists and agnostics see those in the Republican Party becoming more extreme, while white evangelicals see the Democratic Party as becoming more fringe as each year passes. This is subconsciously conveying the message to Americans that to be religious is to be a conservative Republican, while to be nonreligious is to align with the Democrats and liberals. With each passing year there is less room for anyone to be in the middle. There's certainly no evidence that this trend will reverse itself anytime soon.

SOCIALIZATION

While political differences may be a leading cause of religious disaffiliation, another more basic concern is also worth discussion: social isolation. In 1990, Gallup asked respondents how many close friends they had, outside of relatives. Just seven percent reported having no friends or only one, while 47 percent said they had six or more friends. In 2021, the American Perspectives Survey asked the same question and found dramatically different results. This new survey found that nearly one in five Americans said that they had zero or one close friends while a quarter said that they had six or more.[29] In 2019, the Pew Research Center found that Americans who were at least sixty years old and living alone spent over ten waking hours a day by themselves.[30]

The overall impression that we are left with is that Americans are living more isolated lives today than at any point in our recent history. This is a line of inquiry that has been consistent in the world of social science. Easily one of the most important books written in social science in the past fifty years is by the Harvard political scientist Robert Putnam. In his 2000 work *Bowling Alone: The Collapse and Revival of American Community*, Putnam lays out in painful detail a stunning shift in American society: people are retreating from an active social life. Using mountains of meticulously collected data on membership in organizations like the Lions Club and the Elks Lodge, he shows that America is becoming more socially fragmented. Putnam calculates the share of Americans who bowled in bowling leagues dating all the way back to 1900. He finds that in the 1960s, nearly 8 percent of all adult males bowled in a league, but by the early 1990s, that rate had collapsed to just about 3 percent. The book paints a portrait of increasingly isolated Americans who live on islands far from the rest of society.

The main concern for Putnam is what he describes as "social capital," the invisible bonds that hold a community together. Social capital makes people care about the local school district even when they don't have school-aged children. It's the reason people volunteer to pick up trash on the highway or set up a fundraiser to buy new playground equipment at the city park. Social capital is what gives people a sense of place, purpose, and belonging. With the reported decline in social activities, Putnam worried that the ties that bind people together would begin to fray, and communities would suffer as a result.

Seen through the lens of *Bowling Alone*, the decline in church affiliation and attendance is not unique to just the religious arena but part of a decrease in social activity in all areas of American life. In essence, people stopped joining groups, and church was just caught up in the wave of the desocialization of America. Interestingly, according to Putnam, the main culprit of this social retraction is the introduction of technology, specifically cable television. The book was written in 2000; therefore he was unable to include the full impact of the internet in his work, yet he hinted at the individualizing impact it would have on people's leisure time.[31]

Does the data from the GSS bear out Putnam's conclusions? The GSS asked several questions about social behavior, including how often people socialize with their friends, family, and neighbors, along with a question about how frequently they go to a bar or tavern. I calculated the share of Americans who said that they engaged in each activity at least once a week for figure 2.7. The results are somewhat mixed over the last several years, but it's clear that the social distancing required to slow the spread of COVID-19 had a real impact on the social lives of Americans. Before the global pandemic, Americans spent just as much time with their families today as they did thirty years ago. However, there has been a significant decline in how often

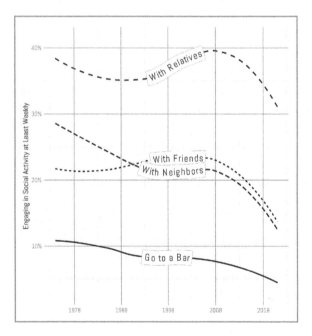

Figure 2.7. Have Americans become less social?

Data from the General Social Survey, a project of the independent research organization NORC at the University of Chicago, with principal funding from the National Science Foundation, https://gss.norc.org/Get-The-Data.

Americans socialize with their neighbors, down from 30 percent to less than 15 percent over four decades. There has also been a noticeable decline in socializing with friends in the last decade. Finally, patronizing bars has dropped almost in half since 1972. So yes, it does seem like Americans are less social now than they were in the 1970s, but they are still very committed to spending time with their families and almost as likely to spend time with their friends (when a global pandemic is not raging).

The issue that arises with the bowling-alone hypothesis is that it may not have a direct impact on all types of religiosity. As described in chapter 1, social scientists think of religion in terms of behavior, belief, and belonging. If people are more reluctant to engage in social activity, that would likely lead to a decline in religious behavior, specifically church attendance. However, it may not necessarily lead to a drop in religious affiliation because the internet has made it easier to watch church services or religious programming in the comfort (and isolation) of one's home. That trend accelerated dramatically during the COVID lockdowns, when Pew found that nearly 80 percent of religious attenders reported that their church was either streaming or recording their worship services for those who could not attend in person.[32] If Putnam's assertion is true, then the data should indicate a steep drop in religious attendance which could potentially be followed by a rise in religious disaffiliation. The problem with using a theory of social isolation to explain why people leave religion is that the data just doesn't support it.

I calculated the average level of church attendance for two groups in the GSS—the entire sample and a subsample of people who say that they are affiliated with a religious tradition in figure 2.8. While the rise in those with no religious belonging clearly appears in the data, the decline in religious behavior is largely imperceptible. If all respondents are included, the average drop in church attendance over the past 46 years is 20 percent. Just for reference, the nones have risen 24 percentage points in that same time period. If I exclude those who claim that they have no religious affiliation, then the drop is just 12 percent. That means that every four years in America, church

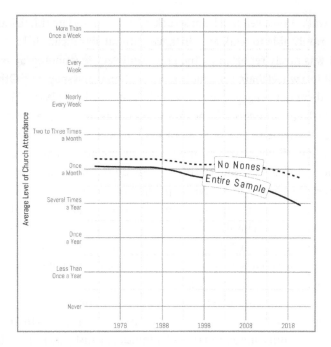

Figure 2.8. Church attendance has not declined significantly.

Data from the General Social Survey, a project of the independent research organization NORC at the University of Chicago, with principal funding from the National Science Foundation, https://gss.norc.org/Get-The-Data.

attendance has dropped a single percentage point. Recall that many of Putnam's measures dropped much more rapidly. In short, this theory of social isolation seems persuasive, but in reality the data doesn't tell such a convincing story.

LOSS OF TRUST

Another force may explain Putnam's data about social isolation: people have lost trust in most societal institutions, including the American government. When Franklin Delano Roosevelt was elected president of the United States during one of the worst economic crises to face the country in its history, he was harboring a secret—he could not walk. Roosevelt had been struck by polio in his late thirties and was rarely able to walk any distance without significant help. This fact was rarely reported by the press, and very few photographs of FDR in a wheelchair were published in national newspapers.[33] Other presidents have engaged in rampant philandering in the White House while the press turned a blind eye. Warren Harding paid secret child support payments to a number of women he had had relationships with. John F. Kennedy had numerous affairs, as did his successor, Lyndon Johnson. None of this ever made the national news.[34] It makes sense that the American public had a great deal of trust in the government for most of the nineteenth century. However, all that changed with Richard Nixon's Watergate scandal. It laid bare for many Americans that the government was being run not by statesmen of noble character and sound decision-making but by morally dubious, self-interested politicians.[35]

Fast forward just a few years, and twenty-four-hour cable news stations MSNBC and Fox News had been on the air for less than two years when Bill Clinton's affair with Monica Lewinsky dominated the headlines and airwaves. No longer would the press turn a blind eye to indiscretion, instead describing the details of leaders' encounters in often lurid detail. The press took on a more investigative role, with many media outlets establishing teams whose role it was to poke and prod every corner of American life. It comes as no surprise that while 77 percent of Americans trusted government to do the right thing at least most of the time in 1964, that share has dropped to 17 percent in 2018.[36] Other scandals soon began to tumble out. As previously noted, in the early 2000s, the *Boston Globe*, along with other newspapers, began to print a series of painstakingly reported stories about how the Catholic Church had systematically been covering up numerous incidences of priests sexually assaulting minors in parishes across the country.[37] Americans were left with a terrifying question: Whom can we trust?

It only makes sense that many people who read the news of the Catholic Church scandal would not only stop attending church entirely but also renounce any religious affiliation so as not to be associated with such activities. Such events are often cited when one reads social media chatter written by people who say that they have no religious affiliation. The data does bear this out, to a point. Not many surveys ask about the Catholic Church's sex abuse scandal specifically, but I found one that was conducted by ABC News in 2002.

The survey asked respondents if they approved or disapproved of the way the church was handling the scandal. A huge majority (nearly 80 percent) disapproved of the way that the Catholic Church was dealing with the problem, which can be seen in figure 2.9. However, the differences by religious tradition are telling. The most support for the church's response unsurprisingly came from Catholics: 28 percent approved. However, just one in five Protestants and just one in ten of the nones approved. The religiously unaffiliated had the strongest level of opposition to the Catholic Church's response. But does this evidence provide support for the theory that the rise of the nones is a direct result of the loss of trust that Americans have in institutions?

The *Boston Globe* ran its first story about the scandal in 2002, so it would seem likely that if this were the driving factor leading

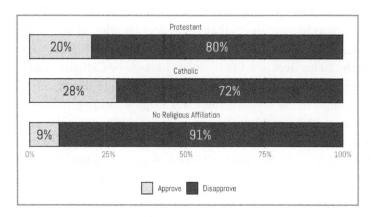

Figure 2.9. How do you feel about the way the Catholic Church is handling the sexual abuse scandal?

Data from ABC News/*Washington Post*, "Catholic Church in Crisis Poll," ICPSR, last modified June 27, 2002, https://tinyurl.com/y5tcg9y8.

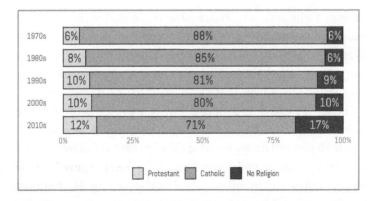

Figure 2.10. In what religious tradition did people raised Catholic end up?

Data from the General Social Survey, a project of the independent research organization NORC at the University of Chicago, with principal funding from the National Science Foundation, https://gss.norc.org/Get-The-Data.

many Catholics to become religiously unaffiliated, then they would have done so soon after the stories began being reported in the United States. The GSS asks respondents about the religion they were raised in, as well as the tradition that they affiliate with as an adult. We would expect to see those taking the surveys in the 2000s to be more likely to defect than in the decades prior; however, that's not what the data indicates. In fact, Catholics taking the survey in the 2000s were just 1 percent less likely to be Catholic as adults than Catholics taking those same surveys before the church was embroiled in the scandal. There was a significant rise in defection between 2010 and 2018. However, this does not support the narrative that the primary driver of disaffiliation was a loss of trust in the Catholic Church, because both mainline and evangelical Protestant defection jumped significantly during this period as well, which is clear from figure 2.9.

I think it's fair to say that the lack of trust that people have in institutions may be a piece of the puzzle, but the evidence does not point to it being the main culprit. It seems plausible that many people have walked away from a religious affiliation since 2000 for a variety of incredibly personal or totally trivial reasons that they may not want (or be able) to describe to survey administrators or their friends and family. Mentioning the Catholic Church scandal may have become an easy way to shut down discussion regarding reasons for leaving religion. I don't want to minimize those who have been affected by sexual abuse in the Catholic or Protestant churches; their stories need to be told, and reforms need to be taken seriously by all religious organizations across the country. But it seems quite a statistical stretch to say that tens of millions of Americans were so affected by the scandal that they left not just the Catholic Church but other faith groups as well.

In the spring of 2022, Paul Djupe, Michael Graham, Jim Davis, and I fielded a survey that was specifically focused on Americans who were dechurched; that is, they once attended church services at least once a month and now report that their attendance is seldom or never. In an effort to understand the causes of people leaving religion behind, we asked a battery of questions about the prevalence of abuse in religious contexts and whether those scandals had a long-term impact on why people were no longer actively attending services. What the data indicates is a great deal of ambivalence when it comes to how the dechurched think about abuse by clergy, as can be seen in figure 2.11.

When it comes to the question of whether the Catholic Church sex abuse scandal did long-term damage to American religion, there's overwhelming agreement among the dechurched that it did, with 71 percent agreeing. However, when asked if children are more likely to be abused in churches than schools or daycares, the plurality of respondents couldn't say either way. That was also the case when they were asked if abuse is more common in Catholic churches than Protestant congregations, or if young people who grew up in a religious household were more likely to face any type of abuse compared to those who grew up without religion. Thus, those who have left religion behind simultaneously agree that the Catholic Church scandal has caused long-term damage to religion in the United States, but they don't seem willing to agree that sexual abuse is widespread in

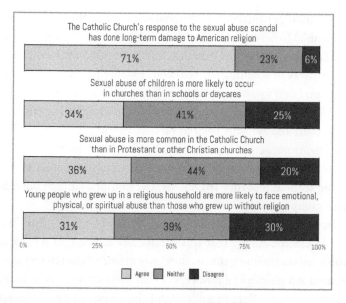

Figure 2:11. Views of abuse among dechurched Americans.

Data from the Great Dechurching Survey. Michael Graham, Jim Davis, Ryan Burge, and Paul Djupe.

religious institutions or that religious households are more likely to subject children to abuse.

CHANGES IN FAMILY STRUCTURE

One other possibility seems worth discussion and that is the fact that the American family does not look the same in the 2020s as it did in the mid-1970s. A raft of social science research concludes that being part of a religious community is more likely when someone comes from a stable household environment. This may be because of a perceived hostility in churches toward single mothers or divorcées.[38] It could be that people see religion as a luxury for people who have a weekly routine, something that falls out of the reach of many Americans.[39] As just one example of that, I calculated the

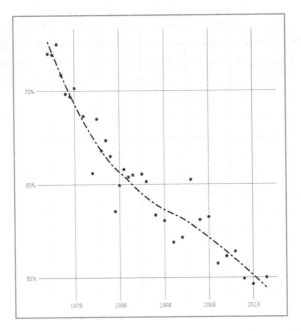

Figure 2.12. The share of Americans who are married has rapidly declined.

Data from the General Social Survey, a project of the independent research organization NORC at the University of Chicago, with principal funding from the National Science Foundation, https://gss.norc.org/Get-The-Data.

share of Americans who said they were married in the GSS dating back to its first iteration in 1972. Figure 2.12 tells a potent story. In the 1970s, nearly three-quarters of all adults in the United States were married. That dropped below half in the late 1990s and has continued a downward trajectory. In 2018, just half of all Americans said they were married. Put another way, if you selected ten random adults in 1972, seven of them would have been married. A random sample of ten adults in 2018 would only contain five married individuals.

While marital status is an important part of the religious affiliation puzzle, it is not the only family-related variable that can drive disaffiliation. One of the most well-cited theories in the sociology of religion is called the "life-cycle effect," which is the understanding that religious attendance waxes and wanes over a person's lifetime.[40] This theory will be looked at in greater detail in chapter 3. But this understanding of religiosity posits that life events like marriage and having children should drive up religious service attendance and affiliating with a faith tradition.

In fact, that is exactly what the data from the GSS shows in figure 2.13: it's clear that the group of people who are most likely to be religiously unaffiliated are people who are not married and do not have children. In fact, 35 percent of that group said they had no religious affiliation in 2018, which is twelve percentage points higher than the rate of the general public. Being married but not having children does make people slightly more likely to be religiously affiliated, with just under 30 percent of this group saying that they

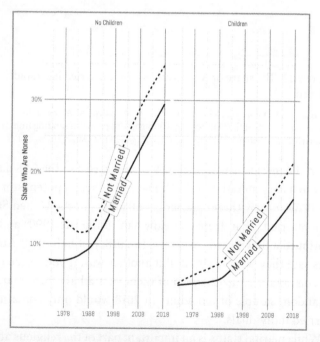

Figure 2.13. The rate of unaffiliated by family status.

Data from the General Social Survey, a project of the independent research organization NORC at the University of Chicago, with principal funding from the National Science Foundation, https://gss.norc.org/Get-The-Data.

were unattached to religion in 2018. However, a larger impact can be seen on the right side of the graph which looks at only people who have children. For those people who have children but are not married, just over 20 percent are unaffiliated, compared to 16 percent of Americans who are married with children. It's worthwhile to note that someone who is neither married nor a parent is twice as likely to be unaffiliated as someone who is both.

It's necessary to point out that while the rate of marriage has dropped substantially in the past forty years, the share of Americans who say they have no children has stayed remarkably stable. The data indicates that the rate of childless adults was approximately 24 percent in the early 1970s but rose to 28 percent by 1990 and has stayed at that level for the past thirty years. The issue is not necessarily fertility; it's family structure. Americans are having as many children as they did three decades ago, but a much smaller share of those children are being raised in two-parent households. However, what clouds this picture a bit is a social science concept called endogeneity. In layman's terms, it means that if we have two variables (in this case religious affiliation and parental status), we can't be sure which one is causing the other to happen.

In figure 2.14, that comes into stark relief. While the prior graph from the General Social Survey (GSS) indicated that those without children are much more likely to be unaffiliated, there's also the counterargument—identifying as an atheist, agnostic, or nothing in particular makes one less likely to have children. The groups that are most likely to have children are religious groups that are often associated with conservative views of marriage and family. For instance, two-thirds of Latter-day Saints between the ages of thirty-five and forty-five are parents; similarly half of Catholic and Protestant households are made up of parents with children. However, the least likely group to have children are atheists and agnostics. Consider this data point: seven in ten atheists who are forty years old are not parents. If there's a reason that I am a bit pessimistic about atheist growth rates it's because the majority of them do not reproduce, which means that conversion is their primary growth channel. But, it's nearly

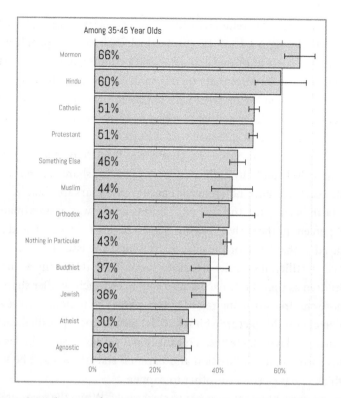

Figure 2.14. Are you the parent or guardian of any children under the age of 18? Among 35- to 45-year-olds.

Data from the General Social Survey, a project of the independent research organization NORC at the University of Chicago, with principal funding from the National Science Foundation, https://gss.norc.org/Get-The-Data.

impossible to untangle the causal arrow between familial structure and religious affiliation. Maybe these atheists left faith behind because they couldn't or didn't want to have children. Or maybe they didn't want to procreate because of their secular worldview.

No matter which way the causal arrow points in this situation, there's strong evidence that religion is being seen more and more as the choice for people who go through life by following the traditional route. For those who get a four-year college degree, marry a partner of the opposite sex, have a well-paying, reasonably satisfying job, and have a few kids—religion is part of their weekly routine. Among those who deviate from that path—whether they have a child outside of marriage, or they get divorced, or a couple decides it would be better to be child free—religion looks less and less attractive. In essence, a religious affiliation lies on the narrow path of people who check all the boxes for the stereotypical "perfect life," which is becoming less and less common as each year passes.

CONCLUSION

To return to the central question of the chapter: Why are the religiously unaffiliated now nearly 30 percent of the population? As with all things in life, it's complicated. I have detailed half a dozen of the most popular explanations, but as I have described, many of them seem to be only partially satisfactory. The problem is that when you combine several of these theories together, the causal arrows hardly ever flow in one direction. Consider what happens when you combine shifts in politics with the just-discussed change in family structure. While it's clear that political liberals are more likely to be religiously unaffiliated, that is also true for people who aren't married and have no children. However, the data from 2018 indicates that Democrats are 10 percent less likely to be married than Republicans. So does one's marital status impact one's politics, or vice versa? The other question that emerges then is how much of the rise in disaffiliation is due to the decline in people being married and how much is related to partisanship? No matter how good a statistical model may be, it can't untangle these difficult causal problems.

If I had to point to a few factors, I think that secularization, politics, and the internet are the major causal factors that have given rise to the nones. It seems foolhardy to believe that Europe, a continent that is very similar to the United States in terms of educational attainment and economic growth, could see a massive decline in religious affiliation and that somehow the United States would avoid that same fate, at least to some degree. I do believe that America is a stubbornly

religious country in ways that Europeans cannot adequately understand and social science can't completely explain. What that means
is that I don't believe we will ever see a time where huge majorities
of Americans are unchurched. However, to try to pinpoint where
the march of the nones will end is a fool's errand.

While secularization might have put the pieces in place for America's disaffiliation, I think what accelerated the shift were changes in
politics, fueled in no small part by the introduction of the internet. In
every graph that looks at American religion, something unmistakable
happens in the early 1990s. While the nones were slowly trending
upward to this point, their rise accelerated dramatically around 1995.
The biggest religious trend occurring at that moment was the rise
of evangelicalism and the religious right. Recall that evangelicals
hit their high-water mark in 1993, when they were 30 percent of the
population. It doesn't take a huge causal leap to believe that as the
loudest and most numerous voices in Protestant Christianity became
more theologically and politically conservative, that drove off a lot
of moderates. To make matters worse, evangelicals have continued
to drift to the right side of American politics since the 1990s. The
GSS always asks people to place themselves on a seven-point scale of
partisanship that ranges from "strong Democrat" to "strong Republican," with "Independent" as the middle option. In 1990, 43 percent
of evangelicals identified as Democrats; today, just 27 percent do.
As evangelicals have become more linked to one political party,
that has naturally led to the alienation of a lot of people who think
differently about politics.

I don't think any amount of rhetoric from social scientists or
theologians will convince tens of millions of evangelicals to veer
back to the theological and political center in the coming decades.
Websites that derive millions of clicks per month focus on making
the other side of the religious or political debate look silly. Human
beings want to have their beliefs about the world confirmed. In many
ways, the damage has already been done—the wave of the nones
will continue to grow in size. However, what I think is unquestionably valuable is for both people of faith and those who claim no

religious affiliation to understand the contours of this ever-growing bloc of American society. While each of the nones arrived at the same place through their own journey, it's helpful to understand what they hold in common—socially, politically, and demographically. What follows is a deep statistical dive into the world of the religiously unaffiliated.

CHAPTER 3

The Demographics
of Disaffiliation

The prior two chapters have been focused on how the nones have grown so large and some possible explanations for their growth, but another question looms—Who are the nones? We all generate stereotypes in our heads when we think of groups of people; it's just how our minds work. It's easy to create a caricature of what an atheist or agnostic looks like: a young white male who spends a lot of time on internet forums calling Christians "sheep." Or a philosophy professor at a liberal arts college who wears a tweed jacket with elbow patches and tries to convince undergraduates that Nietzsche really was right—God is dead. However, you'll find that both of those mental images are fairly inaccurate once you look at the data.

Here's a reality that most people don't fully appreciate about the religiously unaffiliated. In 1972, just one in twenty Americans said that they had no religion. When a group is that small, it can be fairly homogeneous. The way that most groups grow (religious or not) is through personal connections, not because of grand, macrolevel shifts in philosophical or political sensibilities. To declare that you were a none in 1972 was to align your identity with a group that was very much the minority in American society. It took a tremendous amount of conviction to make such a declaration. For most people, publicly declaring a shift in religious affiliation just wasn't worth the social cost.

In 2022, about three in ten Americans said that they didn't affiliate with a religious tradition. That means that about 75 million people in the United States would choose the "no religion" option if they took the General Social Survey (GSS). There is no way a group can grow that large without becoming much more diverse. That's why it's nearly impossible to give a simple description of who the nones are: they exist in large numbers in age, income, and educational spectrums. They now reflect the racial diversity of Americans as a whole and are more gender diverse than ever before. And while many people assume that the religiously unaffiliated are far-left political liberals who favor the Democratic party, that's become less and less true every election cycle.

In short, the nones look like the United States because they make up such a large part of this country. However, what that also means is that any strategy of evangelizing the religiously unaffiliated cannot be one-size-fits-all. In fact, my hope is that a lot of pastors and denominational leaders will come away from this chapter with the realization that they had no idea what the nones really look like. The data indicates that they come from all walks of life and represent what could accurately be described as the largest mission field in the United States today.

AGE-PERIOD-COHORT ANALYSIS

It's tempting to say that the growth of the religiously unaffiliated is a product of youth. That is, every successive generation has a larger share who are unaffiliated than the last, and this provides a straightforward justification for the steady increase of the nones. This explanation has the benefit of being somewhat true, but it is also incredibly oversimplified. The problem with age is this: it's an incredibly difficult theoretical concept to wrap your mind around. In fact, because of its complexity, social science has generated an entire methodological approach to this problem called age-period-cohort analysis. It's best to explain it by way of an example.

Everyone who lives to a full life expectancy will pass through all the typical age milestones. For instance, all Americans will become adults at eighteen, be able to gamble and buy alcohol at twenty-one, and be eligible to run for president at thirty-five. In this simple example, we are discussing just the biological concept of aging. People age and their hair begins to gray, they become more susceptible to disease, and their interests and hobbies begin to shift. I would venture to guess that when someone thinks of aging, this is what comes to mind.

However, that a person turns thirty-five may not have the same psychological and social impact in 2022 as it did in the past. Consider a thirty-year-old woman who was born in 1930 versus one born in 1980. According to the US Census Bureau, that hypothetical woman born in 1930 celebrated her thirtieth birthday and her tenth wedding anniversary around the same time. For the woman who entered the world in 1980, there's a good chance she was still unmarried at age thirty, or if she had tied the knot, they would still be in the honeymoon phase.[1] Couple that with the fact that the average age of first-time moms has jumped nearly four years since the 1970s and it becomes clear that turning thirty today means something entirely different from what it did just a few decades ago.

To take this into account, social science has coalesced around the concept of a birth cohort, which usually means placing people who were born in a five-year time frame into a group that can be analyzed over their entire lives. By creating these birth cohorts, social science can to some extent control for the fact that people move through the life course at different rates today compared to the way they did in the past. Obviously, there are going to be outliers. Even today, some people get married straight out of high school, while others never decide to head down the aisle. But cohorts help social scientists generate coherent pictures about how the process of moving through life impacts different generations in different ways.

However, what throws a wrench into this whole tactic is what have been called "period effects." We know that not all years are created equal. Most go by without any sort of national or international event that will register on our psychological and sociological world. However, some time periods change the way that we think about the world in dramatic ways.

My grandmother Emma was born in 1912. She was seventeen years old when the stock market crashed, and she transitioned into adulthood when the United States was going through the worst economic depression seen in a century. It deeply affected the way that she saw the world. She never put more than an inch of water in the tub for bathing, and anything more than a five-second look in the refrigerator without grabbing something drew a harsh scolding for wasting electricity. She lived frugally because it had been necessary for her to survive. However, someone born just fifteen years later or earlier would not have been molded by economic struggle in the same ways.

Period affects account for the idea that there are specific moments in American history that can have a measurable effect on sociological behavior. Events like the Civil War, Pearl Harbor, the conflict in Vietnam, Watergate, and the September 11 attacks all changed the way that Americans think about themselves, their existence, and America's place in the world. Despite the fact that these events occurred when the members of a single birth cohort were roughly the same age, they each may have been shaped by these events in completely different ways. For example, those who were drafted in Vietnam and those who weren't may have vastly different outlooks on war and peace.[2] When the Twin Towers fell in 2001, I had just graduated high school and I personally know several young men and women who enlisted in the armed forces in the surge of patriotism that followed the terrorist attacks. For many of my classmates who signed up to defend the United States, their experiences in Iraq and Afghanistan changed the course of their lives forever. That's a classic example of a period affect.

The problem of understanding how the natural aging process and the reverberations of national or international events influence people sociologically is especially hard to disentangle when trying to understand American religion. As previously discussed, being an atheist in a deeply religious part of the country in 1980 was an entirely different reality from being in that same situation in 2019. The advent of the internet and social networks has had differential impacts on people's views on faith, religion, and spirituality. A Catholic who was raising young children in the church when the sex abuse scandal became national news likely had a different reaction from one who had no children or was far removed from the concerns of parenthood. September 11, 2001, drove a lot of people to return to church, but its long-term affect on religious behavior is statistically negligible. Seismic events like these can create outliers in the data concerning religious behavior and affiliation.

With that as context, I visualized the distribution of age in the seven religious traditions that were described in detail in chapter 1 as well as the distribution for the entire sample. Figure 3.1 represents data from 1972 through 1980 as a beeswarm plot. Where the plot gets wider, that represents a larger number of respondents bunched up around that age group. In addition, I included the average age for each faith tradition at the top of its plot. Note how that fatter part of the distribution for the entire sample is fairly wide at the bottom, which is reflective of the fact that 36 percent of adults were under the age of thirty-five in the 1970s. Many other traditions mirror this distribution. For instance, 35 percent of evangelicals and 39 percent of Catholics were in this age group as well. That is a strong indicator of the growth potential for these traditions, as these adherents are in peak fertility. But the numbers for the nones are clearly an outlier. Nearly six in ten of the religiously unaffiliated were under the age of thirty-five in 1972–80. No other faith tradition had above 45 percent of its adherents in that cohort.

However, things shift when the sample is restricted to just 2008 through 2018. Most notably, every tradition has gotten older because Americans have gotten much older in the past four decades. That's largely a function of fertility rates undergoing a slow and predictable decline. It's unlikely that we will see another baby boom in the near future. As a result, the distribution of age looks much different today. For instance, the largest bulge for evangelicals used to be under the

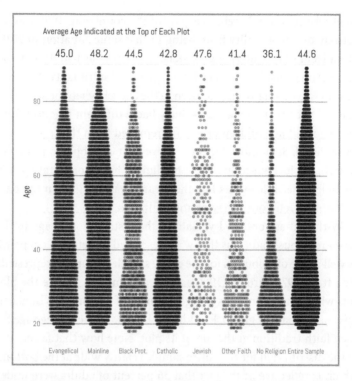

Figure 3.1. The age distribution of each tradition from 1972 to 1980.

Data from the General Social Survey, a project of the independent research organization NORC at the University of Chicago, with principal funding from the National Science Foundation, https://gss.norc.org/Get-The-Data.

age of forty, but no more. Now the wide part of the distribution is between the ages of forty and fifty. The shift for mainline Protestants is even more dramatic. Now the average mainline Protestant is 57.4 years old—an increase of 9.2 years, easily the biggest shift of any group. However, the nones have gotten older as well. The average religiously unaffiliated American is now six years older today than they were in the 1970s, which is larger than the median increase in age for all Americans. Said another way, America is getting older, but the nones are getting older more rapidly.

While 59 percent of nones were under the age of thirty-five in the first graph, that has dropped to 40 percent in the past decade, which is visualized in figure 3.2. At the same time, the share of the unaffiliated who are at least sixty years old has jumped from 10 percent in the 1970s to 19 percent since 2008. However, it would still be statistically inaccurate to say that the prototypical none is now starting to sprout a few gray hairs. The modal age for a none in the 1970s (meaning the age that shows up the most in the distribution) was twenty-three years old. In the more recent data, the modal is still just age thirty-three—which is four years younger than the modal age of the average American. That's a small shift when compared to evangelicals.

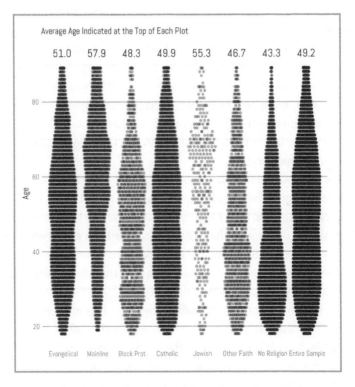

Figure 3.2. The age distribution of each tradition from 2008 to 2018.

Data from the General Social Survey, a project of the independent research organization NORC at the University of Chicago, with principal funding from the National Science Foundation, https://gss.norc.org/Get-The-Data.

The modal age of an evangelical in the 1970s was twenty-four years old. Today, the age that appears the most among evangelicals is fifty-eight. For mainline Protestants the modal age is now sixty-seven years of age. So it's fair to say that the nones have gotten older, but that was inevitable given the trends going on in American society. The larger concern for Christians is that their median age is climbing quickly, and with fewer young people to pack the pews with children, that could lead to a membership cliff in the coming decades.

However, there are other ways to look at the relationship between age and religious affiliation. As a way to get closer to the issue of birth cohorts, I grouped the sample into four generations: the Silent Generation (1925–44), baby boomers (1946–64), Generation X (1965–76), and millennials (1977–95). I then calculated the share of each generation that described itself as unaffiliated in each wave of the GSS, dating back to 1972 for figure 3.3. Because of how age interacts with these generational categories, millennials don't appear until the late 1990s, when the oldest of them moved into adulthood. I have not included Generation Z in this graph because only a small handful of them have reached adulthood so far, but there will be more on them in the next section.

The Silent Generation is obviously the least likely to say that they have no religious affiliation. However, that's not to say that they haven't seen some changes in their religious affiliation over the last five decades. From the 1970s through the 1990s, the share of this group who said that they were nones stayed very low—hovering around five percent. That began to change around 2000, when their trend line slowly began to creep up. By 2008, about eight percent of the Silent Generation were nones, and that reached double digits by 2014. This may be because the oldest members of this generation were dying off by 2010 and those who were left were born in the late 1930s and early 1940s. The data indicates that at least one in ten of this generation are nones now.

The baby boomers show a progression that is completely unique to their generation. When the GSS began in 1972, the oldest baby boomers were just finishing high school, so the first portion of their trend line depicts the turbulence of youth. Note that about 13 percent

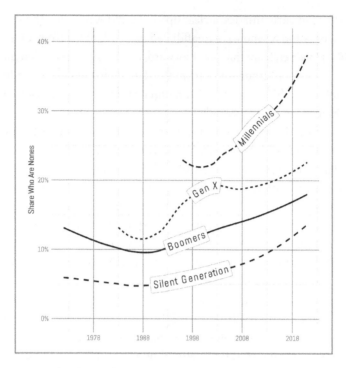

Figure 3.3. The share of each generation that is religiously unaffiliated.

Data from the General Social Survey, a project of the independent research organization NORC at the University of Chicago, with principal funding from the National Science Foundation, https://gss.norc.org/Get-The-Data.

of them said that they were unaffiliated in the early 1970s, but that figure actually dropped below 10 percent in the late 1980s, when many of them were getting married and starting families. However, from that point, the trend line rebounds and shows a steady upward trajectory. According to the most recent data, about 18 percent of boomers are now unaffiliated.

That same trough is also apparent for Generation X but can be statistically deceiving. In the late 1980s, just a small fraction of Generation X had moved into adulthood, so the sample size included just the leading edge of Gen X. When all of them move into their twenties or early thirties, a clear upward trend is present. The share of Generation X who were unaffiliated nearly doubled from 1998 to 2003. However, from that point forward, the line has almost flattened out. The overall impression from the data is that about one in five members of this generation is unaffiliated, which is still below the average for the entire sample.

The same little trough that appeared around 1988 for Generation X appears about fifteen years later for millennials, when the oldest millennials were entering adulthood. But as more of them moved into their twenties, the line begins an unmistakable climb upward. It's notable how clear the data points are for the past decade, generating an incredibly consistent trend line. From 2012 to 2018, the share of millennials who were unaffiliated jumps 2.8 percentage points. But in just the three years from 2018 to 2021, the share of millennial nones jumped six percentage points. I will discuss why I think there was such a significant increase in chapter 5. Projecting these trends into the future is risky business, but with a trend that is so consistent, it seems safe to say that we have not seen a plateauing of the millennial nones. Just to put some clear numbers on this, in 2021, 20 percent of baby boomers, 23 percent of Generation X, and 39 percent of millennials were nones. The jump from Generation X to millennials is staggering in size—a full fifteen percentage points.

As previously mentioned, Generation Z was left out of the previous analysis because of a small sample size. However, the Cooperative Election Study (CES) does contain a much larger number of this youngest generation (over three thousand), affording us the ability to gauge how they are affiliating—or not—with religion in the United States. As can been seen from figure 3.4, there are tremendous differences in how the Silent Generation and Generation Z declare their religious identity, which portends a much different future for faith in the United States.

Among the Silent Generation, half identify with a Protestant tradition while another 22 percent are Catholic. On the other hand, 18 percent identify with no religious tradition. Said another way,

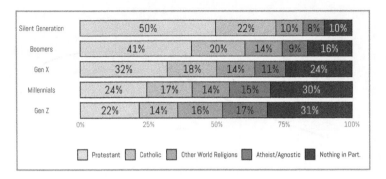

Figure 3.4. Religious breakdown by generation.

Data from Stephen Ansolabehere, Brian F. Schaffner, and Sam Luks, Cooperative Congressional Election Study, Cambridge, MA: Harvard University, http://cces.gov. harvard.edu.

for every member of the Silent Generation who is a none, there are four Christians. Among each successive generation, there are fewer Protestants and Catholics and more atheists, agnostics, and nothing in particulars. For instance, half of Generation X are Christians, while 35 percent are nones. The balance begins to switch among millennials, with 30 percent saying that they are nothing in particular and another 15 percent describing themselves as atheists or agnostics. In comparison, 41 percent are Protestant or Catholic. However, from a statistical perspective it would be unwise to say that the nones clearly outnumber the Christians among the millennials.

Among Generation Z, the difference between the nones and Christians is large enough to be both statistically and substantively significant: just 22 percent of Gen Z are Protestants and 14 percent are Catholics—36 percent of total Christians. That's just slightly larger than the share who say that they are nothing in particular at 31 percent. But once the atheists and agnostics are added (17 percent), the total share of nones among Generation Z rises to 48 percent, clearly much larger than the share who are Christians. Thus, there's ample reason to believe that the future of America is one in which half of Americans have no religious affiliation.

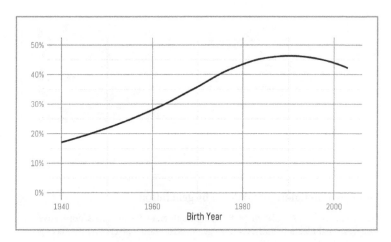

Figure 3.5. Share who are nones by birth year.

Data from Stephen Ansolabehere, Brian F. Schaffner, and Sam Luks, Cooperative Congressional Election Study, Cambridge, MA: Harvard University, http://cces.gov. harvard.edu.

All this said, there's also some evidence that the share of nones will plateau at that level. In figure 3.5, I calculated the share of each individual birth year who identify with no religious tradition in the 2021 CES. Because of a small sample size, the analysis begins with people who were born in 1940—which means that they were in their early eighties when responding to the survey. Among the oldest Americans, about 18 percent said that they were nones. The portion who are religiously unaffiliated rises above 30 percent among people born after 1962 and gets to 40 percent among those who were born after 1975. But, note what happens in those born between 1980 and 2000—the trend line flattens out, if not turning down just slightly among the youngest adult Americans. I am not willing to go so far as to say that the percentage of nones will decline among young people moving into adulthood, but I think it's fair to conclude that the nones will not rise exponentially for the foreseeable future. There's somewhat of a ceiling on this percentage, between 45 and 50 percent, that doesn't look easy to overcome.

One more essential piece of the puzzle is found by sorting people into five-year birth cohorts instead of generations. This helps zero in on period effects; while the oldest millennials were twenty-four when the Twin Towers fell, for example, the youngest were just six years old. After dividing the GSS into sixteen birth cohorts, the sample was clustered into six age ranges. The purpose of this is to understand if being thirty years old in 1980 has the same impact on religious affiliation as being thirty years old in 2000. One of the primary understandings of how religion works is called the life-cycle effect. In short, scholars have long assumed that an individual's religiosity does not move in a clear, linear direction as they move through each of the significant life stages. Instead, the assumption has long been that religiosity looks more like a roller coaster—rising at certain parts of one's life, while declining during other sections. Figure 3.6 visualizes these changes. In childhood, many people experience their most intense period of religiosity. That's likely because parents often force young people to go to church frequently and church camp, mission trips, and other youth-oriented activities give young people many opportunities to think deeply about religious matters. However, when one moves into young adulthood, there's a tendency for college aged people to seek out their own identity separate from their parents and religiosity tends to wane during this time in one's life. As one moves into their late twenties or early thirties, things begin to settle down. Many get a stable job, get married, and have children. Because many people want to raise their children in a similar manner to their own upbringing, they return to religion.

However, as those toddlers slowly turn into teenagers, then eventually graduate high school and move out of the home, that leaves the parents with an empty nest and a difficult choice: are they going to church because they enjoy it or were they going because they wanted to set a good example for their own children? This leads to a divergence in paths. Some redouble their efforts in a religious community, finding meaning and purpose in volunteering and serving their congregation. Other folks get near retirement and move away from those types of commitments, with many leaving religion behind. A cohort analysis

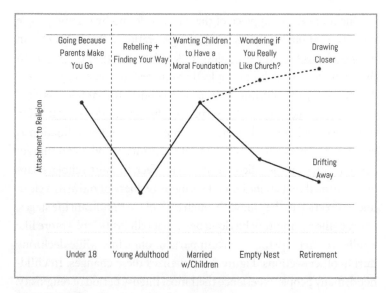

Figure 3.6. The life-cycle effect visualized.

This is just hypothetical data I made up to visualize the life cycle effect.

is an ideal way to determine if this up and down pattern is occurring among those who have been through many of these key life stages.

While the first few graphs in the first row of figure 3.7 don't afford us the ability to see how individuals in those birth cohorts moved across the entire age range, the second row begins to reveal some interesting patterns as people age. For those born between 1940 and 1944, the line is essentially flat across the life course—meaning age had no impact on their rates of disaffiliation. However, there is a very slight uptick as this age group has moved into retirement. But that begins to change for those born in the 1960s. Many in this birth cohort seemed to stay fairly close to religion as they aged through their mid-thirties, but then as they crossed into middle age, the percentage of nones began to move up somewhat. That appears to be the case among those born in the late 1970s as well. In essence, what this analysis reveals is that the older these people got, the more likely they were to walk away from religious affiliation. Thus, while the life-cycle theory seems to make sense, there's little evidence in the data of any peaks or troughs in religiosity across

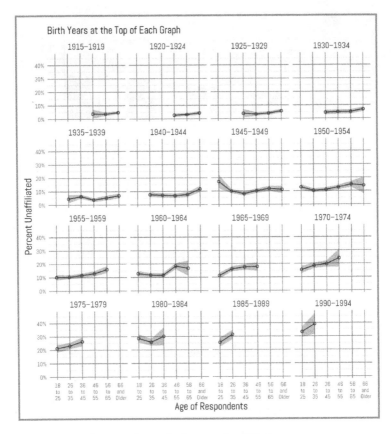

Figure 3.7. Cohort analysis of religious disaffiliation.

Data from the General Social Survey, a project of the independent research organization NORC at the University of Chicago, with principal funding from the National Science Foundation, https://gss.norc.org/Get-The-Data.

the life course. Instead, people just become less religious as they age. There's no empirical reason to believe that millennials came back to church in their thirties, for instance. But what may be easily missed when looking at this graph is that the *y*-intercept keeps going up. In other words, more people are entering adulthood without a religious affiliation, and they become more likely to stay a none as they age.

To put a finer point on this, figure 3.8 visualizes the share of each birth cohort who indicated that they were raised without a religious

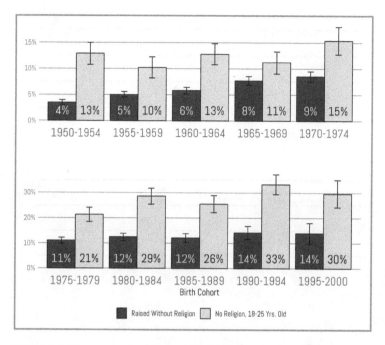

Figure 3.8. Share raised without religion/have no religion as young adults.

Data from the General Social Survey, a project of the independent research organization NORC at the University of Chicago, with principal funding from the National Science Foundation, https://gss.norc.org/Get-The-Data

affiliation. Among those born in the 1930s and 1940s, just three percent were raised with no religion in their home. This percentage stays below five percent until we move into those born in the 1960s, when those raised without religion move up to about seven percent. Among those born in the 1970s, one in ten had no religion in their household growing up. But among those who were born in the 1990s, 14 percent were raised with no religious tradition. And, as was seen in figure 3.6, there's evidence that this provides the baseline for disaffiliation as these young people work through their first decade of adulthood.

Even so, note how much disaffiliation jumps from the share who were raised without religion to those who claimed no faith in early adulthood. In almost all cases, the share who are nones by their twenty-fifth birthday is double the rate of those who were raised without religion in the first place. Consider that among young people in the 1990s, 14 percent had a nonreligious household but nearly a third said that they were nones by their mid-twenties. So, household faith is a part of the puzzle, but a tremendous amount of disaffiliation happens in young adulthood as well.

As can probably be ascertained, age and time are difficult concepts to try to untangle methodologically. However, there seem to be a few clear messages that emerge. One is that the patterns that manifested themselves for the baby boomers and the silent generation are not that instructive when trying to understand religion among today's young people. Dozens of books on church growth have tried to glean insights from the way the baby boomers drifted in and out of a religious community, but the reality is that this was a unique moment in American history, and strategies for evangelizing millennials shouldn't be based on the findings derived from prior generations.

The other clear outcome is that no singular seismic event nudged Americans back toward a religious affiliation or toward becoming a none. Instead, the shift toward disaffiliation was gradual and unrelenting. It's clear that every successive generation starts out less religious than the one prior, but that's only a part of the puzzle. As these young people become more outspoken about their move away from religious affiliation, it gives permission to older people who had been sliding toward disaffiliation to finally declare their true religious attachments. If this is truly the case, then many more nominal Christians are going to check the "no religion" box going forward, and that's not necessarily true just among the youngest Americans.

EDUCATION

Recall that the preeminent sociologist Max Weber believed that education was antithetical to religion. Most well-educated European countries have been described as post-Christian because very few of their citizens see religion as an important part of their daily lives. As such, we would expect to see a similar pattern in the United

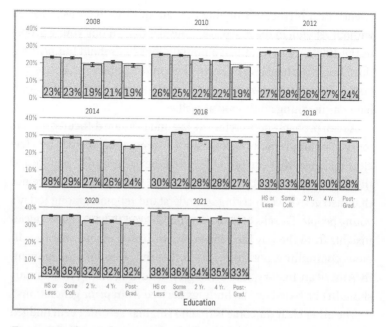

Figure 3.9. Share who are nones by level of education.

Data from Stephen Ansolabehere, Brian F. Schaffner, and Sam Luks, Cooperative Congressional Election Study, Cambridge, MA: Harvard University, http://cces.gov.harvard.edu.

States: more educated Americans disaffiliating from religion in larger numbers than those who had lower levels of educational attainment. Fortunately for social science, that's an easy theory to test given that nearly every survey includes a question about educational attainment.

The Cooperative Election Study (CES) has been conducted yearly since 2008, and recall from chapter 1 that it provides three options for an individual to declare that they have no religious affiliation: atheist, agnostic, and nothing in particular. Figure 3.9 visualizes eight different years of the CES, broken down into five categories of educational attainment ranging from a high school diploma or less to a post-graduate education. In every single wave of this survey, those with the lowest level of education are more likely to say that they have no religious affiliation than those with the highest level of education. While this percentage varies from survey to survey, it averages four to five percentage points less among those who went beyond a four-year college degree. Thus, while Weber and Marx both believed that education would push people away from a religious affiliation, the data refutes that.

To put an even finer point on this, I analyzed data from the Nationscape survey, which was administered by the Democracy Fund. This survey was put into the field every week from July of 2019 through January of 2021. The average size of each wave of the survey was nearly 6,200 respondents. When aggregated together, the entire dataset is 477,255 respondents. For comparison, the average horse race poll that is reported on during the run-up to a presidential election is a thousand respondents. What that means practically is that despite the fact that those with a doctorate represent a very small fraction of the American public, there are over nine thousand of them who responded to the Nationscape survey.

In figure 3.10, we can see the same general pattern that was visualized through the thirteen waves of the Cooperative Election Study (CES)—there is a negative relationship between education

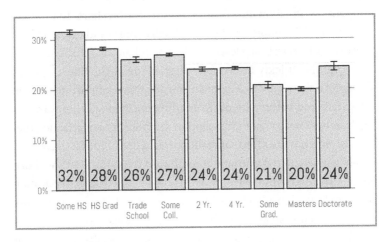

Figure 3.10. Share who are nones by education.

Data from the General Social Survey, a project of the independent research organization NORC at the University of Chicago, with principal funding from the National Science Foundation, https://gss.norc.org/Get-The-Data.

and declaring no religious affiliation. In the Nationscape survey, 32 percent of those who did not earn a high school diploma identified as nones—the highest percentage of any educational level. Among those who finished a high school diploma, just 28 percent were nones. Among those who went to college or trade school, the nones percentage drops—especially among those who earned an associate's or bachelor's degree. The group least likely to be nones in the Nationscape data were those who took some graduate courses or earned a master's degree—one in five of them said that they were an atheist, agnostic, or were attached to no religion in particular. It is worth pointing out that those with a doctorate were more likely to be nones at 24 percent. However, that's no different than those with a college degree, and four points lower than those who only finished high school.

The prior analysis may be missing a bigger piece of the puzzle: that the impact of education may have varied based on birth cohort. Consider the fact that just 5 percent of adults twenty-five and older had a bachelor's degree in 1940, but today that share has increased to 33 percent of adults. That indicates that earning a bachelor's degree may mean something entirely different today than it did four decades ago, and that rates of religious disaffiliation may depend more on birth cohort. To test that, I broke the GSS sample into five-year birth cohorts and calculated the share of each educational level who had no religious affiliation.

As can be quickly inferred from glancing at the line graphs in figure 3.11, there's not a clear and unmistakable relationship between education and being religiously unaffiliated. Said another way, this analysis does not provide clear support for Weber's secularization theory. However, it does find some support in a few of the birth cohorts. For instance, there is a pronounced upward trend line for those born in the latter half of the 1940s, so in this cohort, it is true that education and secularization are related. This is also somewhat evident for those born between 1940 and 1944 but in a more muted way.

However, younger Americans (meaning those born in 1955 or later) seem to have a much flatter trend line, meaning that the relationship between higher levels of education and religious disaffiliation is nonexistent or very small. For instance, there's not a single birth cohort after 1970 in which those who have done some graduate

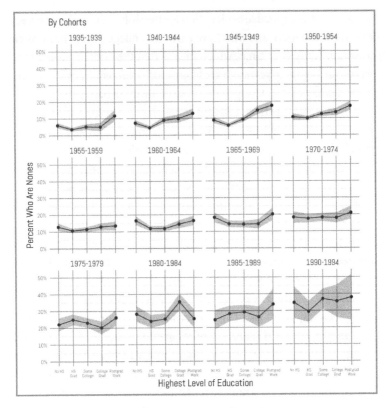

Figure 3.11. Relationship between age and nonaffiliation.

Data from the General Social Survey, a project of the independent research organization NORC at the University of Chicago, with principal funding from the National Science Foundation, https://gss.norc.org/Get-The-Data.

work are statistically more likely to be unaffiliated than those who dropped out of high school.

Thus it's fair to say that if one meets a fortysomething with a master's degree, they are no more likely to be a religious none than someone they graduated high school with who didn't decide to pursue further education. These results provide only very minimal support for the idea that education and religious affiliation are negatively related. While that may have been somewhat true for generations that were born before 1950, the mass disaffiliation that appears in the data for those with college degrees largely abated in the last few decades.

Let me offer a possible explanation for the shift. As previously noted, the share of Americans who have earned a college degree has grown astronomically over time, which means that the type of people who went to college fifty years ago are likely much different from those who are attending classes today. A university education used to be reserved for those who came from upper-middle-class backgrounds, who may have been more inclined to shift away from religion anyway. Now people from all walks of life are earning bachelor's degrees. So while it still may be true that some people are lured away from religion after taking a few college philosophy courses, that's the exception, not the rule.

Before moving on, it's important to document how education impacts the other aspects of religiosity that were described in chapter 1—belief and behavior. To do that, I analyzed the relationship between education, attendance, and belief in God from the last ten years of the General Social Survey (GSS). The results are visualized in figure 3.12. The left panel is the percentage of each educational group that reported that they never attended church services. The data indicates that if there is a relationship between education and religious behavior, it's a negative one. This means that at higher levels of education people are less likely to report never going to services than people who have a high school diploma or less. It's important to note that the size of this effect is fairly small at about five percentage points. Still, it would not be accurate to say that educated people are less likely to show up to church on Sunday morning.

However, when it comes to religious belief, a different pattern emerges. The GSS asks respondents what they believe about God and are given six response options ranging from "God doesn't exist" to "I believe in God without a doubt." The right panel of figure 3.12 is the share of people who took the atheist position (God doesn't exist) or the agnostic one (There's no way to find out God exists). There is evidence here that higher levels of education do point toward a greater propensity to take the atheist or agnostic position. While only 8 percent of high school graduates take this position on God, it's 16 percent among those with some postgraduate education.

To summarize this section, the evidence that education leads people away from religion is mixed, at best. In fact, there's clear

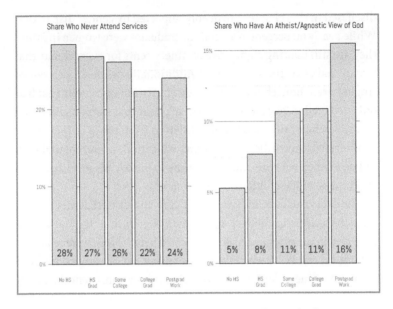

Figure 3.12. Share who never attend services / Share who have an atheist/agnostic view of God.

Data from the General Social Survey, a project of the independent research organization NORC at the University of Chicago, with principal funding from the National Science Foundation, https://gss.norc.org/Get-The-Data

and unmistakable evidence that people who have completed a college degree are less likely to say that they are atheists, agnostics, or that they have no religion in particular compared to those with a high school diploma or less. The data also indicates that those with a higher level of education are more likely to attend religious services than those with a lower level of educational attainment. However, in the case of religious belief, there is evidence that those with higher education are more likely to express a skeptical view of God's existence.

GENDER

What is, so far, an unexplored component of the rise of the nones is gender. Obviously, many of the demographic variables that have been discussed in this chapter are deeply impacted by gender disparities. While nearly 60 percent of all college graduates were women in 2016,[3] they are still making eighty-five to ninety cents for every dollar that a man makes in the workplace.[4] Additionally, while 86 percent of single-parent households were headed by a woman in 1960, that had only declined to 76 percent in 2011.[5] It's clear that women's financial and time constraints look much different from those of their male counterparts, regardless of income, education, or parental status. But do women who are often struggling to make ends meet and raise children sacrifice religious commitment?

The data visualized in figure 3.13 clearly indicates that they do not. That characteristic "hockey stick" style of growth of the nones that appeared in my prior analysis is replicated here. Things were relatively flat until about 1990, when the rates of disaffiliation jumped for both men and women. And what is startling is how consistent the gap is

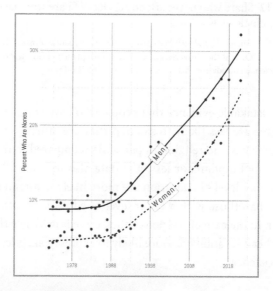

Figure 3.13. Disaffiliation by gender.

Data from the General Social Survey, a project of the independent research organization NORC at the University of Chicago, with principal funding from the National Science Foundation, https://gss.norc.org/Get-The-Data.

between the two groups throughout the 1970s and 1980s: it's roughly five percentage points during this time period. But as time passes, both groups disaffiliate more frequently, and the rate of disaffiliation for men begins to outstrip that of women. Between 2012 and 2016, the gap has stood somewhere between seven and ten percentage points. However, the most recent data collected in both 2018 and 2021 shows the gender gap narrowing. In 2018, 26 percent of men were nones and 21 percent of women. In 2021, the difference between men and women was also six percentage points (32 percent for men and 26 percent for women). Thus both genders are walking away from organized religion, but the clear consensus is that men are doing so at even higher rates.

One potential explanation for the religious disaffiliation gap between genders may be related to child-rearing. As previously mentioned, women are three times more likely to be in single-parent households today than men, which means that many more of them are faced with the question of whether they should make religion a part of their children's lives. As mentioned in chapter 1, having children can be a factor that helps limit the rate of religious disaffiliation, but what role does this play in keeping women in religious traditions? To test that, I broke the sample down by gender as well as by whether the respondents had children. Additionally, I limited the analysis to people under the age of fifty to concentrate only on those who would be wrestling with these issues related to child-rearing and religion.

Figure 3.14 is a fascinating look at the interplay between gender and parental status. It comes as no surprise that people without children are much more likely to have no religious affiliation than those who have children. In fact, nearly four in ten men who had no children in 2018 were a religious none, compared to just 27 percent of men with children. The gap for women was even larger—39 percent for childless women versus 20 percent for women with children. However, something peculiar has happened in recent years among the childless—the gender gap has closed. More specifically, the difference in religious disaffiliation rates for men and women without children has shrunk to zero in 2018 (although the trend lines haven't caught up yet). For those with children, the gap is much

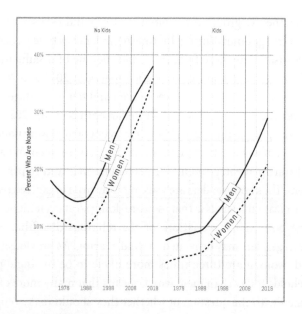

Figure 3.14. Disaffiliation by gender and parental status.

Data from the General Social Survey, a project of the independent research organization NORC at the University of Chicago, with principal funding from the National Science Foundation, https://gss.norc.org/Get-The-Data.

larger—nearly 9 percent. But comparing the two groups of women reveals a staggering fact—while 20 percent of women with kids were a none in 2018, the rate of disaffiliation among women without kids is 38.5 percent. In essence, a childless woman is twice as likely to be a none. For men, the gap is significant as well (eleven percentage points), but smaller than women.

This is worth some consideration. As noted previously, marriage and children are key touchstones that typically bring people back into religious communities. Marriage as an institution has declined significantly as part of a typical life course for younger Americans. However, the data indicates that while fewer people are getting married every year, the share of Americans who do not have children has stayed remarkably stable. That means that the vast majority of individuals who choose to be childless are making a conscious decision to pursue a lifestyle that stands in opposition to the dominant culture. It takes no huge theoretical leap to assume that this decision is much more difficult for a woman to make than a man. Consider the fact that until 2008, a majority of women said that they preferred staying home and taking care of their family, and just 56 percent of women in 2019 preferred a job outside the home.[6] A willfully childless woman has to fight against a great variety of societal pressures, many of which emerge from traditional religious beliefs about gender roles. Thus, these women may feel even greater relief when walking away from religion, as they are no longer subject to messages that try to undermine their lifestyle choices.

There's one more way to think about how gender and religion interact that is worth consideration. The Cooperative Election Study (CES) has a sample that averages thirty thousand respondents, giving us the ability to analyze the data both by gender and age and still have thousands of respondents at each interval. I wanted to understand if younger men were more likely to be nones than younger women, or if age and gender interact differently when it comes to religious disaffiliation. The results of that survey between 2016 and 2021 are visualized in figure 3.15, with the birth year of respondents on the x-axis.

In 2016, we still see a noticeable gender gap in respondents—specifically, women are less likely to say that they have no religious affiliation than men at the same age. However, it's noteworthy that this gap begins to narrow among respondents born in 1990 or later. In the next two years, that same general pattern is visible, though there is some reason to believe that young women are at least as likely to be nones as men. By 2019, it becomes clear the youngest men in the sample (born around 1995) are less likely to say that they are nones than men born in the late 1980s. This appears in 2020 and 2021 as well, giving us more evidence that it's not just a one-year statistical aberration. At the same time, there is no downturn in the share of the nones among the youngest women. Instead, their line continues to rise, even among the very youngest women in the sample. The result? There's clear evidence here that young women are more likely to be nones than young men.

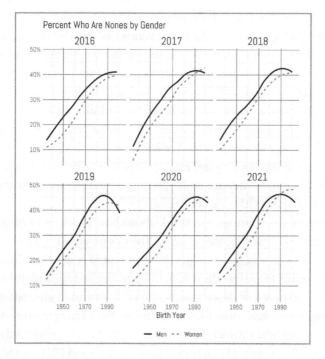

Figure 3.15. Percent who are nones by gender.

Data from Stephen Ansolabehere, Brian F. Schaffner, and Sam Luks, Cooperative Congressional Election Study, Cambridge, MA: Harvard University, http://cces.gov. harvard.edu.

This represents a seismic change in how academics think about issues related to gender and religious affiliation. I also analyzed religious service attendance rates among men and women, and the same pattern emerges—young women are going to church less frequently than young men. Scholars of American religion have operated under the assumption that men were less likely to be religious than women. It's likely that academics will have to update their view of this in light of the last few years of data and go in search of reasons for why the gender gap has essentially flipped. There's no easy answer right now. Some of it may be that young women are being turned away by the views of many churches on issues like gay marriage, abortion, or women in leadership. And there's always the possibility that these young women may come back to religion as they move into other stages of life that can include marriage and childbearing. It's too early to know at this juncture, but if this trend does not abate, it will have serious impacts on the future of American houses of worship.

RACE

As is the case with gender and religion, there is also a significant social component to race and religion as well. For most of the history of the United States, white Christianity was the dominant religious tradition. However, that has slowly begun to change as factors related to immigration and secularization have significantly altered American society.[7] For many racial groups, there is a strong cultural connection to a religious tradition. For instance, despite the fact that many Latinx have been in the United States for generations, they often still have a strong familial connection to a religious tradition.[8] Likewise, Black American culture has always placed a great deal of emphasis on Protestant Christianity.[9] However, those who trace their ancestry back to the Eastern religions of Asia have a different cultural sensibility from those with other racial backgrounds.[10] Because of these differences, the level of cultural acceptance of religious disaffiliation varies widely.

While the GSS only offers three racial options (white, Black, and other), the larger CES provides many more, including white, Black, Hispanic, Asian, and several other options. It also allows respondents to specify whether they are an atheist, agnostic, or "nothing in particular," as was previously mentioned in chapter 1. This affords us tremendous insight into not just the rate of religious disaffiliation by racial group but also what label people choose when they leave organized religion.

It's clear from figure 3.16 that Asians are an outlier compared to the other racial groups. In 2008, they were 10 percentage points more likely to be religiously unaffiliated than any other racial group. That upward trend has continued, and now over four in ten Asians have no religious affiliation. The other racial groups (white, Black, Hispanic, and others) land much lower than the Asian sample. For instance, 23 percent of whites were nones in 2008; that has jumped to 36 percent by 2021,

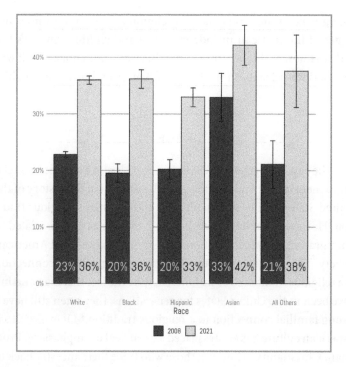

Figure 3.16. Share who are nones by race, 2008 vs. 2021.

Data from Stephen Ansolabehere, Brian F. Schaffner, and Sam Luks, Cooperative Congressional Election Study, Cambridge, MA: Harvard University, http://cces.gov. harvard.edu.

which is right in line with the overall sample mean in the 2021 CES. Hispanic disaffiliation is more modest. In 2008, just 20 percent were nones; now the share is 33 percent, an increase of thirteen percentage points. What might be the most surprising racial group is Black Americans, however. In 2008, they were one of the least likely racial groups to be religiously unaffiliated (20 percent). In just a thirteen-year time period, the rate of disaffiliation has jumped a staggering sixteen percentage points to 36 percent. It seems possible that the share of Black people who are nones might double in less than fifteen years.

One aspect of religious disaffiliation that deserves a closer look is the interaction between race and partisanship. As was discussed in chapter

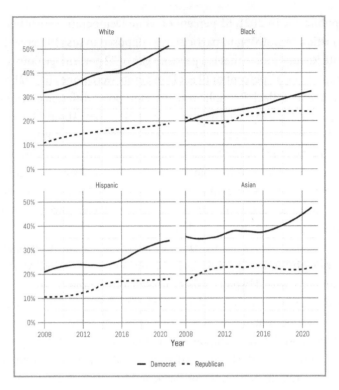

Figure 3.17. Share who are nones by race and partisanship.

Data from Stephen Ansolabehere, Brian F. Schaffner, and Sam Luks, Cooperative Congressional Election Study, Cambridge, MA: Harvard University, http://cces.gov. harvard.edu.

2, there's ample reason to believe that politics is driving many people away from religion in the United States. The fact that over 40 percent of politically liberal individuals are nones compared to just about 10 percent of political conservatives is empirical support for this phenomenon. But when the interaction of race and political partisanship is combined, there's strong evidence that both factors are crucial to understanding the rapid rise in religious disaffiliation, as can clearly be seen in figure 3.17.

The first difference that leaps out is the top left panel of figure 3.17, which focuses only on white respondents. In 2008, 32 percent of white Democrats were nones compared to 10 percent of white

Republicans. In 2021, 51 percent of white Democrats were atheists, agnostics, or nothing in particular, as opposed to just 19 percent of white Republicans—that is a partisan gap of 32 percentage points. In comparison, 33 percent of Black Democrats were nones in 2021 and 23 percent of Black Republicans, just a ten-point difference. Among Hispanics, the gap is relatively small in 2021 as well. About 34 percent of Hispanic Democrats were religiously unaffiliated compared to 17 percent of Hispanic Republicans. In 2021, an Asian Democrat was twice as likely to be a none compared to an Asian Republican (48 percent vs. 24 percent). Thus, there's evidence here that there are clear racial differences in the nones that are exacerbated when political partisanship is added to the mix.

These differences are worth dwelling on just a bit. It's probably most helpful to group white respondents with Asians and African-Americans with Hispanics, based solely on the partisan gap that exists when it comes to the share who are nones. For both white and Asian respondents there is a strong connection between being a Democrat and being religiously unaffiliated (about 50 percent for both groups). Among both racial groups, just 20 percent of Republicans also identify as nones. For Black and Hispanic respondents, it's still very easy to be a Democrat while also identifying with a religious tradition. Two-thirds of both Black and Hispanic respondents still identify with a religious tradition. Thus, among these groups, there's not such a strong "God Gap"—it's still possible to vote for Democrats and also identify as religious. That's increasingly not the case for white or Asian respondents.

However, while looking at nones as a general category provides a good starting point, digging into which label they choose can provide a window into how culture impacts religious disaffiliation. The three options of atheist, agnostic, and nothing in particular provide respondents the freedom to indicate whether they have truly walked away from religion to become an atheist or agnostic or just don't feel strongly about religion and fall into the nothing-in-particular category. As you can see in figure 3.18, this distinction does make a difference for some racial groups.

A significant number of white nones are comfortable with claiming an affiliation that is far from theism. In fact, nearly four in ten white nones are atheists or agnostics—the highest share of any racial group. On the other end of the spectrum are Black people. Black Americans are reluctant to totally reject religion, with just eight percent of Black respondents identifying as agnostic and only six percent claiming to be atheists. Consider this: a white none is two and a half times more likely to be an atheist or agnostic compared with a Black person. The cultural forces that shape religious choice in minority communities look much different from those among white Americans. Words like "atheist" and "agnostic" may carry a

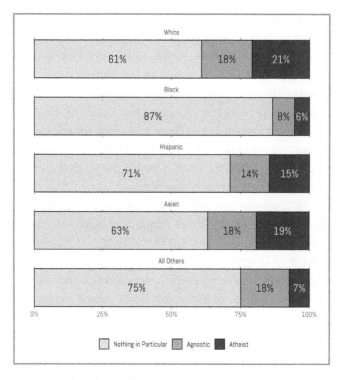

Figure 3.18. Types of nones by race.

Data from Stephen Ansolabehere, Brian F. Schaffner, and Sam Luks, Cooperative Congressional Election Study, Cambridge, MA: Harvard University, http://cces.gov. harvard.edu.

lot more baggage for someone in the Black community compared to someone who is white or Asian, for instance. We will dig more deeply into the various types of nones in the next chapter.

CONCLUSION

Taken together, the data paints a chilling picture. There is no segment of American society that has been immune to the rise of religious disaffiliation. While it would be easy to say that this is largely driven by young people moving away from a religious faith, there's also some evidence that older Americans are moving away from faith communities as they enter their twilight years. While churches used to rely on many of their young people moving back toward a religious tradition when they hit their thirties and forties, that seems to be less and less likely with each successive generation.

The data indicates that less-educated Americans are only slightly less likely to move away from religion than those who have at least some college education, but as more and more Americans pursue course work at the collegiate level, the likelihood of disaffiliation does increase. At the same time, many of the societal factors that used to keep women in church have begun to fade. In 2018, a woman without children was just as likely to be a none as a childless man. That portends a bleak future for religion, as more Americans are choosing to be child-free. Some of the cultural influences that surround religion among racial groups have diminished as well. The rise in disaffiliation among Black Americans is alarmingly rapid, and now there is no racial group that is not at least 30 percent religiously disaffiliated.

I think comparing American churches to a styrofoam cup filled with water is an appropriate analogy. Churches have always had pinholes punched in the sides of their cups. They would lose water through the deaths of their older members, but the water kept being replenished by young families bringing their children or by members converting people from the community. For many, the water being poured in vastly exceeded the amount that was lost through the pinhole-sized leaks. Now those small drips have become gaping holes, and the water is leaving rapidly. Those holes represent a rapidly aging core demographic that is dying off, but those punctures also include those who grew up in the church but then left, never to return. At the same time, the flow of water that used to refill the cup has slowed to a trickle as churches continue to struggle to bring in new members.

If the flow of water into the cup slows down even more or the holes expand in diameter, the cup is going to run empty at some point in the near future. But all is not lost. The next chapter will focus on the three types of nones—atheists, agnostics, and nothing in particulars. If the church wants to increase the flow into its cup, there are potentially large reservoirs in the American population, some of which seem fairly easy to tap. Other data may also point toward ways to reduce the size of the holes that have formed in their cups. If less water flows out the bottom and more pours in from the top, churches can maintain their congregations far into the future.

CHAPTER 4

Nones Are Not
All Created Equal

One of the most memorable trips of my college experience was a long weekend in Chicago as part of the required curriculum at Greenville College. The goal of the trip was simple: expose college freshmen to a broader range of religious expression than they likely experienced growing up. I can honestly say that it changed my life. The first stop was at an Episcopal Church. As someone who had grown up Southern Baptist, I had no experience with the mainline tradition. Things only became more awkward when I realized that the priest who was going to conduct the service and serve Communion was a lesbian. As she gave me a sip of real wine (the first alcohol to touch my lips), I knew that I could never tell my very evangelical grandmother about my experiences in Chicago.

The weekend only became more disorienting from there. We attended a Catholic mass at a large cathedral, and we sat in a synagogue and heard a rabbi read the Torah in Hebrew on Friday night. We wrestled with the similarities between Christianity and Islam while visiting a mosque. I will never forget the sense of awe, wonder, and silence that pervaded the Bahá'í House of Worship as I stared up over one hundred and thirty feet to the top of their temple on the North Shore of Chicago. Before we boarded the buses to return to downstate Illinois, we also worshipped at St. Benedict the African

Catholic Church, which features a truly unique combination of Catholic liturgy and Pentecostal song and dance.

I still wrestle with some of the things I saw, heard, and felt while on that three-day trip. But one thought that struck me immediately as we drove back home through the cornfields was that religion is so incredibly diverse that I will never truly be able to understand it all.

The same may be even more true for the various ways one can be religiously unaffiliated. Up to this point, I have largely treated all the nones as a single social group. Obviously, that's a total oversimplification. In fact, lumping all of them together is just as inaccurate as trying to analyze all Christians as a single group. My trip to Chicago made that painfully clear to me.

In some ways, the religiously unaffiliated are the most difficult group to characterize in American society. At least Christians can agree that the Bible is a sacred text and that a worship service should contain some songs, Scripture reading, and prayer. The religiously unaffiliated are not a cohesive group in the same way. The reality is that the only thing that truly binds them together is the fact that they might all check the same box on the survey form.

What makes matters even more difficult is that the General Social Survey (GSS), which I have been using extensively in the last few chapters, affords only that one box for the nones: "no religion." That places someone who actively tries to convert people away from religion in the same category as someone who just doesn't think about matters of faith that much at all.

However, I have another data source that does allow for a deep dive into the different types of religiously unaffiliated Americans. The Cooperative Election Study (CES), which surveyed over sixty thousand people in 2021, indicates that 32 percent of Americans are Protestants, while 36 percent are religiously unaffiliated. The Protestant group is further divided into seventy denominations. The religiously unaffiliated are broken down into three categories: atheists, agnostics, and nothing in particular. Clearly, those three options for identifying as a none are still unduly reductive, but they can provide more nuance than the one category that exists in the GSS.

Despite the fact that all the nones are lumped into just three groups, a great deal of insight can be extracted from these three categories. After analyzing these three groups for the past few years, I have developed a clearer picture of the nones. Obviously, an atheist has an entirely different outlook on religion, politics, and their place in the world from someone who merely selects the "nothing in particular" option. These choices have huge ramifications for denominational leaders and potential evangelists who wonder what type of people would be receptive to an invitation to attend a church service or openly talk about matters of faith.

What follows is a brief description of each of the three none groups, followed by some basic demographics to provide some broad details about the differences between atheists, agnostics, and nothing in particulars. Finally, I will discuss the religious characteristics of each group. The data tells a clear and unmistakable story: nones are not all created equal.

ATHEISTS

It's fair to say that when someone talks about the "nones," their minds likely jump to atheists. Often in discussions, I hear pastors and other religious leaders use the term *atheists* as a catchall for people who are not attached to a religious tradition. In many ways, atheists are an atypical, slightly extreme version of nones. As was discussed in chapter 1, atheists make up about 6 percent of the adult population of the United States—just one in five of all the nones. So while they are obviously vocal on internet forums, they don't speak for the majority of the nones.

The data indicates that there's a great deal of anti-atheist sentiment among the American public, so to choose the term *atheist* on a survey means to accept all the baggage that comes with that term. The 2012 American National Election Study asked respondents to rate their attitudes toward twenty-two groups on a scale ranging from 0 (meaning very cool) to 100 (meaning very warm).

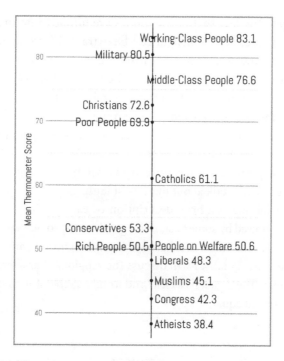

Figure 4.1. Thermometer score of various groups.

Data from the American National Election Study, "2012 Time Series Study," https://tinyurl.com/y2rncj8l.

The average score for some of those groups is visualized on a single line in figure 4.1.

Working-class people do very well, scoring 83.1 on a scale from 0 to 100. Just behind them is the military at 80.5. Christians as a whole score 72.6, while Catholics come in about ten points lower at 61.1. Atheists are at the very bottom of the graph. The mean score for this group is 38.4, which is four points lower than the United States Congress. The religious group that is the closest in score to atheists are religious fundamentalists, and they are more than ten points higher at 49.1. Clearly, there's a great deal of anti-atheist bias in the United States, so to voluntarily take on that moniker is to invite possible ridicule and ostracism. As such, atheists tend to be the most militant in their belief system.

AGNOSTICS

The term *agnostic* dates back to 1869, when Thomas Henry Huxley, the right-hand man to Charles Darwin, used it in a speech to describe his view of the supernatural. It comes from the Greek term *gnosis*, which means "to know" and, when combined with the prefix *a-*, indicates an uncertain view of the supernatural. Huxley stated, "It simply means that a man shall not say he knows or believes that which he has no scientific grounds for professing to know or believe."[1]

As such, agnostics are a step removed from the certainty that is espoused by atheists, who clearly believe that there is no Higher Power in the world. Often agnostics will use the language and construction of reason or scientific inquiry to indicate that because there can be no irrefutable evidence for God's existence, it would be improper for anyone with this worldview to say that God does or does not exist. Instead, agnostics are open to the possibility that either conclusion may be proven empirically true.

Agnostics, as will be described in the remainder of this chapter, are a hard group to understand from a data perspective. Just like atheists, they make up about 6 percent of the adult population. They also sometimes behave in ways that make them seem even more extreme than atheists, while through other lenses, they are much more moderate in belief and behavior. While few surveys ask specifically about people's opinions of agnostics, it does seem likely that they avoid some of the negative sentiment that is linked to the atheist label.

NOTHING IN PARTICULAR

The group that is often forgotten when talking about the nones doesn't have a sophisticated-sounding name like *atheist* or *agnostic*. In fact, this group is unified by a rejection of all labels. When the Pew Research Center asks people about their religious tradition, it gives them twelve options, beginning with the larger traditions like Protestant and Catholic. But after listing both atheist and agnostic, there's one more category: "nothing in particular." This group might be the most consequential religious group in the United States, and no one is talking about them the way they talk about atheists or agnostics. What is a "nothing in particular"? My conception of this group is that when they are asked the survey question about religious affiliation, instead of feeling strongly one way or the other about being attached to a theistic religion—like Baptists, Mormons, or Muslims—or about having no religious inclinations, like atheists and agnostics, they just shrug their shoulders and check the "nothing in particular" box. Note that this is not the same as saying that they are a member of a religious group that is not listed on the survey because the very last option after "nothing in particular" is "something else," which allows people to type their affiliation in a text box. So we know that these individuals are not Wiccans or Jedis. Instead, these are people that just don't feel strongly about religion one way or the other.

A helpful way to think about the distinction between atheists/agnostics and nothing in particulars comes from *Secular Surge*, a recently published book by a team of top political scientists. In it, the authors make a helpful distinction among the nones, between those who are nonreligious (nothing in particular) and those who are secular (atheists and agnostics). Secular individuals have left behind a religious worldview and now utilize a paradigm that is based on logic and science to guide them through life. A statement that a secular person would agree with is, "Factual evidence from the natural world is the source of true beliefs."[2] On the other hand, a nonreligious person is defined by what they are not. They don't go to church, they don't pray, they don't believe that religion is important in their life, but they don't adopt a secular outlook on life either. While seculars have traded in a religious outlook for a secular one, the nonreligious have attached themselves to nothing—they are seemingly floating through life without the scaffolding provided by a consistent worldview.

Nothing in particulars are the definition of the nonreligious and they also happen to be one of the largest religious groups in the United States. If all the nones were represented by just five people, one of them would be an atheist, another one would be agnostic, and three of them would be nothing in particulars. That clearly doesn't fit the image most people have of what the nones look like. In the general American population, nearly one in four Americans is a nothing in particular.

There's an interesting age dynamic when thinking about the three types of nones that are visualized in figure 4.2. About 8 percent of the youngest Americans identify as atheist and about the same percentage say that they are agnostic. Among those who are sixty or older, the share who are atheist or agnostic only drops by about 3 percentage points to 5 percent each. However, there's a much larger age effect for nothing in particulars. Among those between the age of twenty and thirty, nearly a third say that they are nothing in particular. However, among those at retirement age, that percentage drops precipitously to about 15 percent. Thus, there's evidence here that atheists and agnostics are found in near equal measure across the age spectrum, while nothing in particulars are much more likely to be younger. We will explore this from another angle in just a bit.

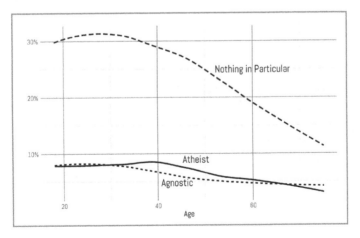

Figure 4.2. Type of none by age.

Data from Stephen Ansolabehere, Brian F. Schaffner, and Sam Luks, Cooperative Congressional Election Study, Cambridge, MA: Harvard University, http://cces.gov. harvard.edu.

While its size alone makes the nothing-in-particular group one to watch, another fact demands that people pay attention to them: they are the fastest-growing religious group in the United States. I visualized the three largest Christian groups: white evangelicals, white Catholics, and mainline Protestants in figure 4.3. Only white evangelicals did not shrink significantly between 2008 and 2021, losing less than a percentage point in thirteen years. At the same time, the nothing in particular group has grown from 14 percent in 2008 to 21 percent in 2021, a full 50 percent increase in size. Remembering in the prior analysis that atheists now make up about 6 percent of the population, while the nothing in particulars have grown by 7 percentage points between 2008 and 2021, we can really put that increase in perspective. In 2021, white Catholics and mainline Protestants

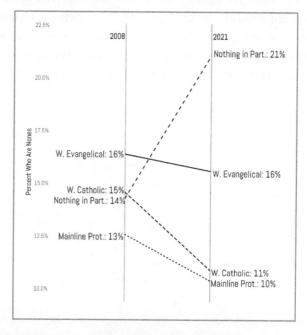

Figure 4.3. Change in the largest religious traditions.

Data from Stephen Ansolabehere, Brian F. Schaffner, and Sam Luks, Cooperative Congressional Election Study, Cambridge, MA: Harvard University, http://cces.gov.harvard.edu.

combined are the same size as the nothing in particular category. It's hard to overemphasize this point, but nothing in particular may be the most important religious category in the United States today.

However, while it is not easy to conceptualize what atheists and agnostics have in common, it's essentially impossible to find any true commonalities among the nothing in particulars. At least atheists and agnostics have a worldview they agree on; the same is not true for nothing in particulars. While the other two types of nones are often antagonistic toward religious beliefs and behavior, the same intensity is not present among nothing in particulars. As the following analysis will illustrate, these are often the most distant, isolated, and checked-out members of society.

AGE

As previously described in chapter 3 and in the previous section, age has a tremendous impact on the likelihood that individuals will disaffiliate from a religious tradition or change their overall church attendance. At the same time, it does not seem to affect the likelihood of their becoming a nothing in particular versus an atheist or agnostic. The average American adult in 2021 was 48.5 years old. In comparison, the nones are about five years younger on average. But the differences in the average age between the three kinds of nones are within the margin of error: for nothing in particulars, it's 43; for agnostics, it's 44.3; and for atheists, it's 44.1. These age differences are almost statistically imperceptible, as is clear in figure 4.4.

About 45 percent of atheists are between the age of 18 and 39 years old. For agnostics, it's a bit higher at 48 percent, while 48 percent of nothing in particulars have not seen their fortieth birthday. The flip side of that, of course, is that at least half of the nones are over the age of forty, so the perception that atheists and agnostics are a bunch of kids in their early twenties trying out something new is just not confirmed by the data. For instance, about 6 percent of the adult population are atheists or agnostics who are at least fifty years

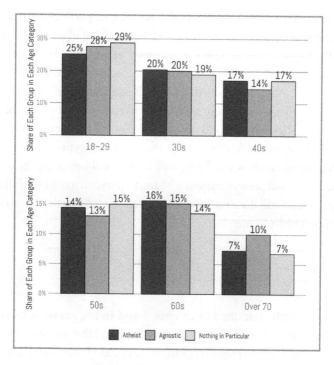

Figure 4.4. Age distribution of the nones.

Data from Stephen Ansolabehere, Brian F. Schaffner, and Sam Luks, Cooperative Congressional Election Study, Cambridge, MA: Harvard University, http://cces.gov. harvard.edu.

old. That 6 percent represents more people than Latter-day Saints, Jews, Muslims, Hindus, and Buddhists combined.

There's something else worth pointing out in figure 4.4, as well. Notice how little the percentages decline once one moves beyond the youngest age group. For instance, 20 percent of atheists are in their thirties, but 16 percent are in their sixties. That same general pattern of modest declines is also evident among agnostics and nothing in particulars, as well. This indicates that there is not a clear negative linear relationship between age and identifying as a none. While there is clearly a spike in nones among the youngest adults, and a smaller percentage of nones who are at least seventy years old, the middle of the age distribution is basically flat. This is further evidence that the perception of the nones as only encompassing younger Americans is not at all reflected in the data.

The question hanging over this analysis, however, relates back to the life-cycle effect that was discussed in the previous chapter. Recall that this theory supposes that religiosity waxes and wanes across the life course. Specifically, when an individual is in early adulthood they will drift away from religion, then come back once they move into a more stable living situation and likely have married and started a family. In this case, it may be that people embrace the atheist moniker when they are younger but then cast it aside as they become more career focused. However, that's not what appears to be happening in the data.

Figure 4.5 examines one five-year birth cohort—those born between 1983 and 1988. This group was selected because they represent those

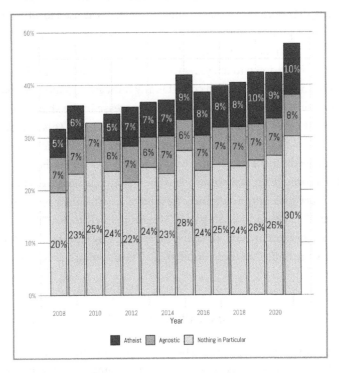

Figure 4.5. Share who are nones among those born 1983–1988.

Data from Stephen Ansolabehere, Brian F. Schaffner, and Sam Luks, Cooperative Congressional Election Study, Cambridge, MA: Harvard University, http://cces.gov. harvard.edu.

most likely to see the seesaw pattern envisioned by the life-cycle effect. In 2008, they were between twenty and twenty-five years old, a prime moment to walk away from a religious affiliation. In 2021, they were between thirty-three and thirty-eight years old, when it's likely that many of them had landed stable jobs and were settling down with a family and/or children. But they are clearly not returning to religion—in fact, it looks like they are joining the swelling ranks of the nones in larger numbers every year. In 2008, 5 percent were atheists. In 2021, that share had doubled to 10 percent. It's noteworthy, however, that the agnostics barely budged during this time frame, only shifting from 7 to 8 percent, which is not a substantively significant change. On the other hand, the nothing in particulars also saw tremendous growth during this thirteen-year window—rising from 20 percent to 30 percent. In total, 32 percent of this birth cohort were nones in 2008. In 2021, it had risen to 48 percent.

Thus, when looking back at the percentages in figure 4.4, it's important to note that it's very unlikely that the share of twentysomething nones will go down in ten years when they move into their thirties. In fact, if the 1983–1988 birth cohort is any indication, a more probable outcome is that there will be a further increase in the share who are nones at every age range as can be seen in figure 4.5. This is a topic I tackled in *20 Myths About Religion and Politics in America*. Chapter 10 focused on the myth that people return to religion later in life. That's something that seems plausible by outside observers but just a cursory look at the data indicates that every five-year birth cohort starting in 1930 and ending in 1994 is more likely to be a none today than they were in 2008. In short, there's not any empirical reason to justify the hope that these numbers will go down in the next decade.

GENDER AND RACE

Here's a quick thought experiment: picture an atheist or agnostic in your mind. What gender are they? I'm going to guess that most people conjure up an image of a man. That does make sense. If you ask people who are interested in atheism to name authors who have had the most profound impact on their religious worldview, many of them will list Sam Harris, Christopher Hitchens, and Richard Dawkins. In July of 2022, I went on Amazon and looked at the top-selling books about atheism. Of the top twenty bestsellers, not a single one was written by a woman. It seems that atheism is largely a male-dominated enterprise—and the data backs that up.

A simple gender breakdown in figure 4.6 provides a clear and unmistakable picture—atheists are much more likely to be male. In fact, just two out of five atheists in 2021 were women. Agnostics have a somewhat more equitable gender distribution, with 47 percent of this group identifying as female. However, the only group of nones where women outnumber men is nothing in particulars, who were 52 percent women in 2021. One has to wonder if atheism will have a hard time growing in the future because most women who convert to that label will have to be persuaded by male authors.

Remember when I asked you to imagine an atheist in your mind? While it's certainly likely that you conjured up a mental picture of a man, it's also very likely that the image you created in your mind was a white male. There's ample reason to justify creating such an arche-type; essentially all the leading thinkers and authors among atheists

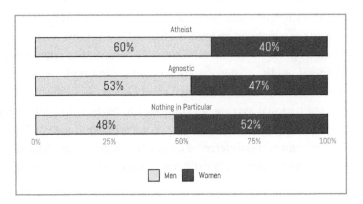

Figure 4.6. Gender breakdown of the nones.

Data from Stephen Ansolabehere, Brian F. Schaffner, and Sam Luks, Cooperative Congressional Election Study, Cambridge, MA: Harvard University, http://cces.gov.harvard.edu.

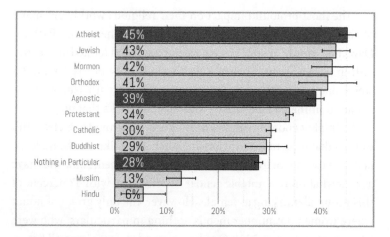

Figure 4.7. Share of each group that is white and male.

Data from Stephen Ansolabehere, Brian F. Schaffner, and Sam Luks, Cooperative Congressional Election Study, Cambridge, MA: Harvard University, http://cces.gov. harvard.edu.

(Hitchens, Dawkins, and Harris) are white guys. But how does the composition of atheist elites reflect atheists in the rank and file? To understand that I calculated the share of every religious group that was both white and male using the 2021 Cooperative Election Study, the results of which can be found in figure 4.7. The most white male-dominated group in 2021 is atheists, at 45 percent. For reference, in the general public, 32 percent are both white and male. Agnostics, while not quite as male-dominated as atheists, are still seven points above the national average. In comparison, nothing in particulars look drastically different at just 28 percent white and male. Clearly, there are tremendous differences among the three groups that can be seen when just looking at two different demographic characteristics.

EDUCATION

Essential to understanding the differences in the types of religious nones is noting just how much they differ in overall level of education. One of the biggest shifts in American life that has gone relatively unnoticed because of how gradually it has occurred is the massive increase in educational attainment by the general population. For instance, in 1972, nearly four in ten Americans had not earned a high school diploma; by 2018, that number had declined to less than one in ten. In addition, many more Americans today have gained a bachelor's degree than in years past. Now 35 percent of Americans have a college degree. But that educational success (and the increased income that typically comes with higher levels of education) has not been enjoyed equally by all religious groups.

Atheists have a very high level of educational attainment, as is apparent in figure 4.8. In 2021, just over half of all atheists had

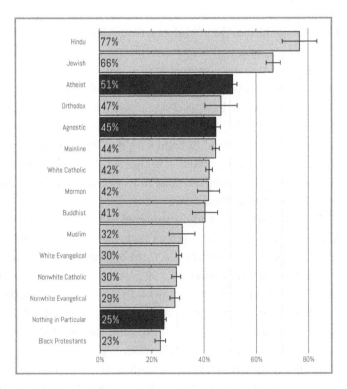

Figure 4.8. Share of each tradition with a bachelor's degree or more.

Data from Stephen Ansolabehere, Brian F. Schaffner, and Sam Luks, Cooperative Congressional Election Study, Cambridge, MA: Harvard University, http://cces.gov. harvard.edu.

earned a bachelor's degree (51 percent). In fact, there is no major Christian group in the United States that can say that they have higher levels of education than atheists. Agnostics follow closely behind atheists, with 45 percent having completed a bachelor's program, which is essentially the same level of education usually attained by mainline Protestants. But to find the last type of nones, the nothing in particulars, you have to move all the way to the bottom of the graph. Just one in four members of this group completed a bachelor's degree, which is ten points lower than the general population. Atheists are twice as likely to have met this academic threshold as nothing in particulars. It's obvious from this angle that nothing in particulars are not demographically similar to atheists or agnostics.

However, looking at the 2021 data provides just a single snapshot of where the nones are now in terms of education. It does not address how their educational attainment has increased over time. While nothing in particulars are clearly at the bottom end of the educational spectrum now, it would be a good sign if their rate of college degree attainment was speeding up over time. To assess that, I calculated the percentage of each type of none with a college degree in both 2008 and 2021, then compared that to the rate of bachelor's degrees in the general public during the same time period. The result of this analysis is displayed in figure 4.9.

In 2008, a quarter of all adults surveyed had earned a four-year college degree. In 2021, that number had risen by ten percentage points to 35 percent. In contrast, a third of atheists had a college degree in 2008, and now that's over 50 percent. That represents an increase of eighteen percentage points. In comparison, agnostics have seen a rise in college degrees that mirrors the general public at about eleven percentage points, but the baseline for agnostics is much higher than the average American. In 2008, 35 percent of them were degree holders. Now, it's 46 percent. Nothing in particulars are the true outlier in regard to the increase in educational attainment. In 2008, just 16 percent of them had completed a college degree, and even in 2021 that had only risen to 25 percent. Or, said another way,

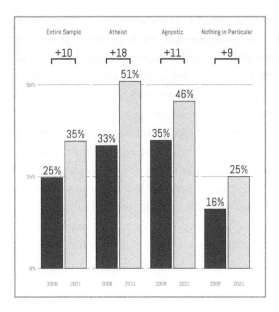

Figure 4.9. Share with a bachelor's degree in 2008 vs. 2021.

Data from Stephen Ansolabehere, Brian F. Schaffner, and Sam Luks, Cooperative Congressional Election Study, Cambridge, MA: Harvard University, http://cces.gov. harvard.edu.

the nothing in particulars lag behind the average person on the street by thirteen years when it comes to educational attainment, while atheists are far outpacing the general public.

INCOME

The impact of this educational attainment on the income of the different religiously unaffiliated groups is profound. For instance, while half of the overall population of the United States earns less than $50,000 per year in household income, 60 percent of the nothing in particulars earn less. That's much higher than the percentage of atheists or agnostics in that bracket. Consider this: a nothing in particular is 50 percent more likely to land in the lowest income category than an atheist. Those differences also appear at the top of the income spectrum in figure 4.10. Nearly three in ten atheists have an annual household income of at least $100,000, while one in five agnostics does. Nothing in particulars lag far behind, with just 13 percent making six figures per year. That is also six percentage points behind the national average.

When education and income are combined, the disparity between the nothing in particulars and the atheist/agnostics comes into full view. To do that, I calculated the share of each tradition who had a high school diploma or less and had an annual household income of no more than $50,000. The results of this analysis are visualized in figure 4.11. Clearly, nothing in particulars are in a completely different part of the social strata of the United States compared to

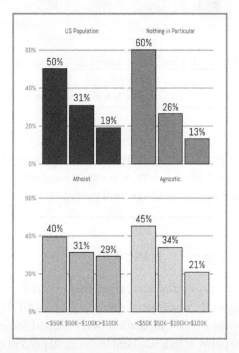

Figure 4.10. Income distribution among the nones.

Data from Stephen Ansolabehere, Brian F. Schaffner, and Sam Luks, Cooperative Congressional Election Study, Cambridge, MA: Harvard University, http://cces.gov.harvard.edu.

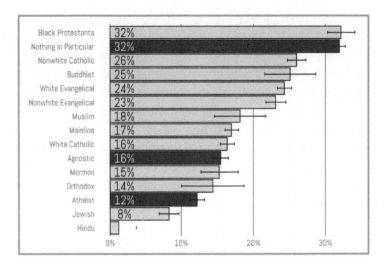

Figure 4.11. Share of each tradition with a high school degree and making $50K per year or less.

Data from Stephen Ansolabehere, Brian F. Schaffner, and Sam Luks, Cooperative Congressional Election Study, Cambridge, MA: Harvard University, http://cces.gov. harvard.edu.

the rest of the nones. Nearly a third of nothing in particulars have low education and low incomes, compared to 23 percent of the public at large. The only group that is comparable is Black Protestants, of whom 32 percent fall into both categories. At the bottom of the graph are atheists and agnostics. Just 12 percent of atheists have no more than a high school diploma and make less than fifty thousand dollars—about half the rate of the country as a whole.

From both an educational and income angle, the data tells an unmistakable story: while atheists, agnostics, and nothing in particulars are all classified as "nones," that term glosses over vast differences in the lifestyles, occupations, and worldviews of these three groups. If anything, this finding underscores the fact that the nothing in particulars are one of the most educationally and economically disadvantaged groups in the United States today, while atheists and agnostics enjoy much higher levels of economic success. But does that play a role in their political behaviors and opinions?

POLITICAL PARTISANSHIP AND IDEOLOGY

Two concepts in political science—ideology and partisanship—help orient groups across the political landscape. Ideology is typically measured on a five-point scale that ranges from very liberal to very conservative, with the midpoint being labeled moderate. Partisanship spans seven points, with strong Democrat on the left side, strong Republican on the right side, and Independent in the middle. While it is true that these two measures are often correlated, many Americans consider themselves conservative Democrats, and there are even a few liberal Republicans in the mix as well. To get a sense of where the three types of nones fall on both dimensions, I generated a scatterplot of eleven different religious groups with partisanship on the horizontal axis and ideology on the vertical axis. The bottom left corner of figure 4.12 would indicate a very liberal strong Democrat, while the top right would be where a very conservative strong Republican would find themselves.

To orient ourselves in political space, I also calculated the mean partisanship and ideology for the entire sample. The average American finds themselves almost smack in the middle of both continuums; however, on partisanship, they are ever so slightly to the left of center. The top right of the graph is filled with the expected groups—white evangelicals and Mormons, but there is quite a bit of clustering around the middle of the graph. A linear relationship can be detected as well. The more a group identifies with the Republican party, the more likely they are to describe themselves as conservative. There are a few outliers on this trend line though. For instance, Black Protestants are the farthest group to the left on the partisanship scale, but they describe themselves as moderates in terms of ideology.

Where do the nones fit into this mix? The nothing in particular group is right in the middle of the graph, not too far from the average for the entire sample. They are slightly more conservative but also slightly more towards the Democratic side of the spectrum. Atheists and agnostics are clearly outliers when it comes to religious groups.

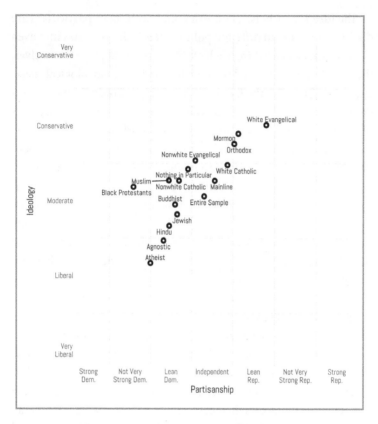

Figure 4.12. Political positions of religious groups.

Data from Stephen Ansolabehere, Brian F. Schaffner, and Sam Luks, Cooperative Congressional Election Study, Cambridge, MA: Harvard University, http://cces.gov.harvard.edu.

Atheists are easily the most liberal political group, with agnostics not far behind. However, on the partisanship continuum, it's fair to say that they are not as solidly Democrat as would be expected. Black Protestants are quite a bit to the left of atheists and agnostics when it comes to identifying as strong Democrats. This analysis makes clear that while religious demographers lump the nothing in particulars, atheists, and agnostics into a single category, there are vast differences in their political viewpoints.

The idea that atheists, agnostics, and nothing in particulars are distinct groups with different political sensibilities comes into even clearer focus when asking each of those groups to place themselves, the Democratic Party, and the Republican Party in ideological space. Beginning in 2016, the Cooperative Election Study asked respondents to do just that, using a scale ranging from 1 (meaning very liberal) to 7 (very conservative), with 4 described as "middle of the road." This is an extremely helpful exercise because it makes respondents think more carefully about what "liberal" or "conservative" really means. If they score themselves a five but place the Republicans at a seven, that means that they see themselves as clearly more moderate than the GOP. It can also tell us if the nones are perceiving the two parties moving away from each other, as well. While social scientists discuss political polarization on a seemingly daily basis, it's not always obvious if the average American can pick up on the fact that the two parties have drifted apart from each other.

In figure 4.13, I've visualized how each of the three types of nones have placed the two major parties and themselves in ideological space. As we can quickly ascertain, there are vast differences among these three groups when it comes to how they view the American political landscape. In the top panel, there's a fairly startling finding: the average atheist now sees themself to the left of the average Democrat. That wasn't the case in 2016, but the gap between the Democrats and atheists slowly began to widen over the next five years. It's notable that atheists believe that the Democratic party has moderated since 2016, while they themselves have become more liberal. I've looked at all religious groups in the Cooperative Election Study; no other group sees themselves to the left of the Democrats, nor does any group see themselves as being more conservative than the GOP. Thus, atheists are clearly a political outlier in the American political landscape.

Agnostics display a bit of a different pattern. In 2016, the average agnostics saw themselves as just slightly left of center, while the Democrats were clearly more liberal in their minds. But the distance between those two groups started to narrow by 2018—the gap was closed by both agnostics moving left and the Democrats moving right. Now, in

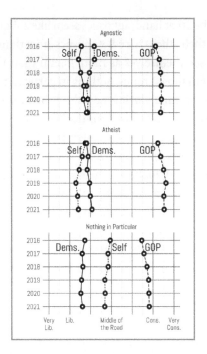

Figure 4.13. Placing groups in ideological space.

Data from Stephen Ansolabehere, Brian F. Schaffner, and Sam Luks, Cooperative Congressional Election Study, Cambridge, MA: Harvard University, http://cces.gov.harvard.edu.

2021, there's no statistical difference in the mean agnostic and where they place the Democratic party. For nothing in particulars, a few things stand out. The first is that they used to see themselves as very much in the middle of the ideological spectrum. In fact, their mean score was 3.96 in 2016. But by 2021, they had crept to the left to 3.68: still moderate, but definitely slightly left of center. In terms of how the nothing in particulars view the two parties—there's not much of a story. They view the Democrats as slightly more moderate than the Republicans and they do seem to think that Republicans have moved more toward the extreme between 2016 and 2021, but not by much.

When figures 4.12 and 4.13 are viewed in their totality, there's ample evidence that atheists are very liberal and are becoming more liberal over time. On the other hand, agnostics seem like a slightly more moderate version of their atheist friend. Agnostics are certainly left of center, but they don't see themselves as more liberal than the Democrats. Compared to both those groups, nothing in particular individuals are much more moderate and moving more slowly in the leftward direction.

One final way to look at the political orientation of the nones may be the most simple and consequential: their voting pattern in presidential elections. In figure 4.14, I calculated the vote share in 2008, 2012, 2016, and 2020 for atheists, agnostics, and nothing in particulars. It should come as no surprise that atheists are overwhelmingly voting for Democrats on election day. Eighty-two percent of them cast a vote for Barack Obama in 2008 and 85 percent supported Joe Biden in 2020. However, while the percentage of the vote hasn't changed much, that doesn't mean the impact of atheists

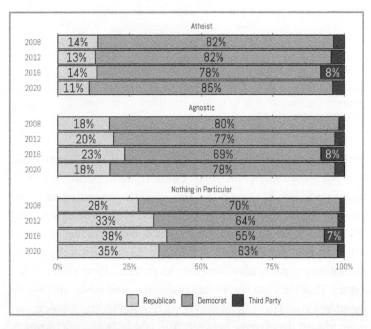

Figure 4.14. Vote choice among the nones, 2008–2020.

Data from Stephen Ansolabehere, Brian F. Schaffner, and Sam Luks, Cooperative Congressional Election Study, Cambridge, MA: Harvard University, http://cces.gov.harvard.edu.

on who wins elections is not being felt. Remember from chapter 1 that atheists were 4 percent of the population in 2008, but 6 percent in 2020. The fact that atheists have gotten noticeably larger while becoming even more unified behind the Democrats translates to hundreds of thousands of votes on election day.

When looking at agnostics, the general impression from the data is relative stability. In 2008, just 18 percent of them favored John McCain. That same share cast a ballot for Donald Trump in his reelection attempt in 2020. Nothing in particulars, however, show much more movement in their voting patterns than atheists or agnostics. In 2008, 28 percent supported the Republican and 70 percent voted for the Democrat. In 2020, 35 percent voted for the GOP, while only 63 percent sided with Democrat Joe Biden. That's a net of seven percentage points for the Republicans over the last twelve years. And recall that nothing in particulars represent over twenty percent of the population now. That means that while the GOP cannot count on this group to help them win elections just yet, they are clearly making in-roads with a large and growing part of the electorate. If the Republicans can continue to chip away at the Democrats' advantage among the nothing in particulars, it will leave the Democrats searching for the votes of other groups on election day.

POLITICAL ACTIVITY

Another dimension to politics merits some discussion when it comes to the nones. While the prior graph indicates that the atheists and agnostics are fairly liberal and lean toward the Democratic party and the nothing in particulars fall somewhere in the middle on both dimensions, that matters little unless those groups are consistently engaged in political activity. Recall that the nothing in particulars had one of the lowest levels of education of any religious group in 2021, with just a quarter obtaining a four-year college degree. On the other hand, atheists and agnostics were some of the most educated people in the United States. How does that translate to the real world of politics? Do atheists and agnostics engage in political activity at a higher rate than the nothing in particulars?

A battery of questions in the 2020 Cooperative Election Study (CES) listed six political activities and asked respondents if they had engaged in that activity in the prior twelve months. I calculated the share of atheists, agnostics, and nothing in particulars who said they did participate in those political activities, as well as visualized the percentage of the general public who participated in those six ways. This illustrates nicely the gulfs that exist among the nones.

First, note in figure 4.15 that atheists are clearly the most politically active none group. Nearly one in five of them attended a protest or

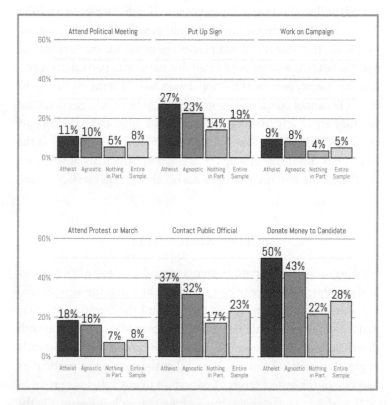

Figure 4.15. Percentage engaging in each political act.

Data from Stephen Ansolabehere, Brian F. Schaffner, and Sam Luks, Cooperative Congressional Election Study, Cambridge, MA: Harvard University, http://cces.gov.harvard.edu.

march, nearly 40 percent had contacted a public official, and over a quarter had displayed a political sign. All those rates are dramatically higher than the general population. Agnostics do not fall far behind their atheist counterparts. Many engage in political activities at a much higher rate than the general public (often just a few percentage points lower than atheists).

Nothing in particulars are an entirely different story. For all six political activities, not only do they engage at lower rates than atheists or agnostics, they also are much less likely to participate than the general public. For instance, just 5 percent of nothing in particulars have attended a political meeting, compared to 8 percent of the general population and 11 percent of atheists. Atheists are two times more likely to attend a protest and nearly twice as likely to donate money to a candidate or campaign.

Obviously, some of this difference can be attributed to the fact that nothing in particulars have much lower levels of education and income, as previously mentioned. However, having a lower socioeconomic status does not preclude people from engaging in political behaviors such as putting up a lawn sign or contacting a public official. On every measure of political participation, they fall far behind. Obviously, the impact of COVID-19 looms in the data when it comes to political activity in 2020. But consider that many of these questions focus on behavior that should have only been minimally impacted by the global pandemic. For instance, contacting a public official requires nothing more than a short email or a phone call. The same is true for putting up a yard sign; often they are given out at parades or campaign offices with minimal physical contact required. Given the volumes of data that indicate Democrats were more likely to comply with CDC recommendations about distancing, it stands to reason that atheists would be the most wary of attending a protest or working for a campaign. But, that clearly wasn't the case in this data. Instead, nothing in particulars, who are much more moderate than atheists or agnostics, were the ones typically on the sidelines of the political process.

RELIGIOUS ATTENDANCE

While the data is clear that the nothing in particular group is much less likely to engage in social activities, such as attending college and political actions like putting up a political sign, does that mean that this group is also more hesitant to darken a church door for Sunday service? Here, the narrative changes somewhat. Looking through the lens of religion brings the picture into focus, revealing that the nothing in particulars as a group seem to be less averse to religious belief and religious activities than either atheists or agnostics. That's clearly true when it comes to how often they attend church, shown in figure 4.16.

It seems logical that atheists would be the least likely to attend services. Prior data indicates that atheists face some negative feelings in the general public, and to take on the label "atheist" means that it is embraced only by those who feel very far away from any type of

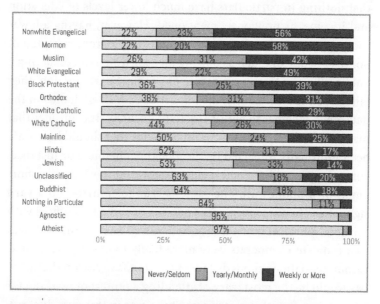

Figure 4.16. Church attendance of different religious groups.

Data from Stephen Ansolabehere, Brian F. Schaffner, and Sam Luks, Cooperative Congressional Election Study, Cambridge, MA: Harvard University, http://cces.gov.harvard.edu.

organized religion. The data corroborates that position. In fact, 97 percent of atheists indicate that they "seldom" or "never" attend church. Agnostics are somewhat more apt to go to church, but not by much. While nearly 92 percent of atheists report never attending, just 74 percent of agnostics do. However, when the "never" and "seldom" responses are collapsed together, 95 percent of agnostics fall into these two categories. Nothing in particulars are more likely to participate in religious services, at least sometimes. In fact, about 7 percent of this group attends yearly, and another 7 percent attend monthly or more. However, 57 percent of nothing in particulars never come to church, and another quarter describe their attendance as "seldom." The data seems to indicate what an outside observer would guess: atheists are the furthest away from a faith tradition while agnostics are somewhat closer, with nothing in particulars having a somewhat higher frequency of church attendance.

There's another element to consider, however, when it comes to religious attendance among the nones. As the previous analysis concludes, atheists and agnostics are very unlikely to attend religious services, while nothing in particulars are slightly more apt to show up to church occasionally. But has that percentage changed over time? Figure 4.17 indicates that the answer to that question is a resounding "yes." In 2008, about 18 percent of nothing in particulars said that they attended services at least once a month. By 2014, that share had risen noticeably to 22 percent. However, from that point forward the percentage of nothing in particulars who attend church monthly has noticeably declined and currently stands at 16 percent—the lowest since 2008. That could mean that nothing in particulars have drifted further away from a religious attachment in the last few years. This, in turn, may mean it would be more difficult for them to return to a faith tradition. That question will be answered with additional data in a few pages.

RELIGIOUS IMPORTANCE

Church attendance is just one aspect of religiosity, as was discussed in chapter 1. Another dimension is religious belief, and while the

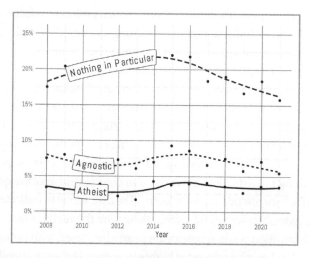

Figure 4.17. Share attending services at least once a month.

Data from Stephen Ansolabehere, Brian F. Schaffner, and Sam Luks, Cooperative Congressional Election Study, Cambridge, MA: Harvard University, http://cces.gov. harvard.edu.

Cooperative Election Survey (CES) did not ask about specific religious doctrines, it did ask, "How important is religion in your life?" In figure 4.18, the same general pattern related to religious behavior seems to be replicated, with some small variations.

For instance, nearly 95 percent of all atheists say that religion is "not at all important" in their lives. That largely tracks what appeared in the prior graph related to church attendance. While that same sentiment is shared by just 76 percent of agnostics, another 19 percent of them say that religion is "not too important." In essence, the difference between these two groups is just a few percentage points. However, we see that nothing in particulars seem to place more importance on religion. For instance, 32 percent of nothing in particulars say that religion is "somewhat" or "very" important in their lives, while at the same time, only 43 percent believe that religion is "not at all important."

From the standpoint of those who are interested in perhaps trying to convert a religious none into a Christian tradition, the data indicates that the group of people who are the most closed off to

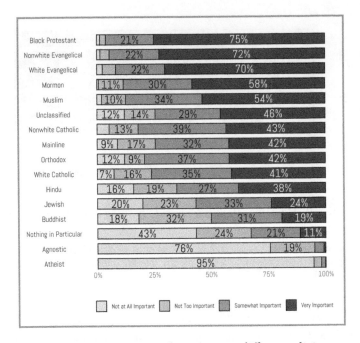

Figure 4.18. How important is religion among different religious groups?

Data from Stephen Ansolabehere, Brian F. Schaffner, and Sam Luks, Cooperative Congressional Election Study, Cambridge, MA: Harvard University, http://cces.gov. harvard.edu.

the possibility of religion are atheists, followed closely by agnostics. Consider the fact that 95 percent of atheists say that religion is "not at all important" and 90 percent of them never attend church. This group is not ambivalent about religion; they actively resist it. Nothing in particulars, on the other hand, seem to be at least somewhat open to the possibility of becoming part of a faith community. Fifteen percent of them attend church at least once a year and a third of them say that religion is at least "somewhat important."

But, again, one has to wonder if the nothing in particulars seem more (or less) open to religion today than they were a few years ago. Figure 4.19 visualizes how nothing in particulars have answered the question about religious importance from 2008 through 2021. The

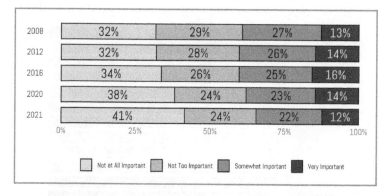

Figure 4.19. How important is religion to nothing in particulars over time?

Data from Stephen Ansolabehere, Brian F. Schaffner, and Sam Luks, Cooperative Congressional Election Study, Cambridge, MA: Harvard University, http://cces.gov. harvard.edu.

results are interesting and present a nuanced picture. For instance, in 2008, 13 percent of nothing in particulars said that religion was very important in their lives. In 2021, that share was 12 percent, not a statistically significant decline. From that angle, it would appear that this group has generally the same view of religion today as they did a decade ago. However, at the other end of the scale, there's a lot more movement. In 2008, 32 percent of respondents said that religion is not at all important. In 2021, that had increased significantly to 41 percent. Yet when not at all important is combined with not too important, the shift is more modest (from 61 percent to 65 percent). Thus, the picture is somewhat cloudy, though it does generally point to the fact that the nothing in particulars are slightly less attached to religion today than in 2008. But does that data mean that conversion is possible?

CONVERSION RATES

The vast majority of surveys in social science are longitudinal. What that means is that the survey administrators randomly poll a group of people every two years. Every wave of the survey represents an entirely new set of randomly selected individuals. This type of survey helps us understand how the size and composition of religious groups have shifted over time, but it does not tell us why those shifts occur. For instance, survey data tells us that about 30 percent of Americans are nones today, but most data sources cannot tell us where they came from. Panel data helps pull back the curtain on those questions. Instead of asking a different set of people a series of questions every two years, a panel survey asks the same questions to the same people more than once over time. While panel surveys are not perfect, they are well suited not only for tracking the shifts in the sizes of religious groups but also for telling us how those shifts occurred.

The CES team did a panel survey that began in 2010 and was followed up in 2012 and 2014. That means that researchers can track how people moved across the religious landscape, jumping from being Catholics or Protestants to nothing in particulars or agnostics to atheists over a four-year period. It provides us an unprecedented look at how the none groups work and how individuals move in and out of these categories as time passes.

To get a sense of how the three types of nones shift their affiliation, I looked at where people who had identified as agnostic, atheist, or nothing in particular in 2010 ended up when they took the final survey in the fall of 2014. The results (visualized in figure 4.20) tell a fascinating story of what American religion really looks like.

For people who were agnostics in 2010, just over half of them were still agnostics in 2014 (55 percent). However, if an agnostic shifted their classification, the group that they were most likely to defect to was atheists, which occurred among a quarter of agnostics. In contrast, just 16 percent of agnostics became nothing in particulars, while 3 percent converted to a non-Christian faith group and 4 percent identified as Christians in 2014. For atheists, the retention rate was much higher. In fact, four out of five people who identified as an atheist in 2010 were still an atheist in 2014. If an atheist did change their affiliation, they most likely moved to nothing in particular, which happened for 13 percent of atheists while another 2 percent became agnostic. However, just 3 percent joined another

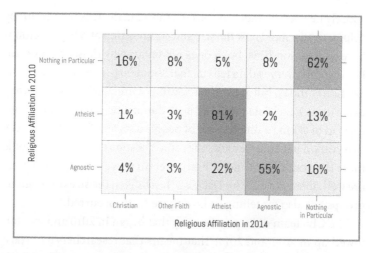

Figure 4.20. How the nones switched identity (2010–2014).

Data from Stephen Ansolabehere, Brian F. Schaffner, and Sam Luks, Cooperative Congressional Election Study, Cambridge, MA: Harvard University, http://cces.gov.harvard.edu.

faith tradition, and less than one in one hundred became a Christian (0.7 percent). Stories of atheists having a dramatic born-again experience seem to be common in evangelical circles but appear in this data to be very rare events.

Nothing in particulars seem to represent something different compared with the other two none groups. Their retention rate is fairly high, with 62 percent still identifying as nothing in particular in 2014, which was somewhat lower than atheists' and just slightly higher than agnostics'. However, where did the nearly four in ten who changed their affiliation over time go? The data says that about 13 percent of them became atheists or agnostics. However, over a quarter of them moved toward a religious tradition. Nearly 9 percent joined a non-Christian faith group, but 16 percent identified as Christians at the end of this four-year period of time.

Admittedly, this data is a bit dated. It's fair to say that a lot changed in the United States between 2014 and now. To see if extending the time horizon on panel data had any noticeable impact on religious switching, I turned to the Democracy Fund, which also administered the previously mentioned Nationscape survey. Alongside that massive collection, they administered a panel study called the Voter Study Group that ran from late 2011 through September of 2020. This gives researchers a nine-year window to track religious change, instead of the four years afforded by the Cooperative Election Study's panel dataset. I conducted the exact same analysis of respondents of the Voter Study Group's nones, the results of which are found in figure 4.21.

The first thing that jumps out is just how consistent the results are between the CES's panel data and that which was collected by the Voter Study Group, despite the fact that the former was a four-year time frame and the latter was nine years. For instance, recall that in the CES data, 4 percent of atheists no longer identified as nones at the end point of the survey. In the Voter Study Group that finding is perfectly replicated. In the CES, 7 percent of agnostics indicated that they were part of a theistic tradition in 2014, and it was 8 percent in the VSG data. The movement of the nothing in particulars

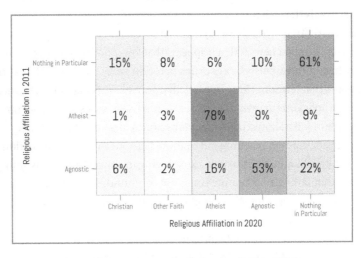

Figure 4.21. How the nones switched identity (2011–2020).

Democracy Fund Voter Study Group. VIEWS OF THE ELECTORATE RESEARCH SURVEY, December 2021. Washington, D.C. https://www.voterstudygroup.org/

is very similar as well. In the CES data, 16 percent of them were identifying as Christians in 2014. In the VSG data, it was 15 percent. In short, there's almost no difference in the results from the Voter Study Group's nine-year sampling window compared to the shorter time frame from the CES.

The fact that these results are nearly identical to each other is worth thinking about a bit more. For a purely methodological standpoint, it's always very reassuring to see two different datasets arrive at nearly the same conclusion. That's strong evidence that one data collection effort is not significantly biased or faulty. But it's also noteworthy that when the time frame more than doubled from four years to nine, that overall switching among the nones did not increase. In fact, when I compared the switching rates of the nones in the 2020 wave of the VSG to the 2016 wave, there was only a handful of differences. What that indicates is that there was a lot more volatility in the religious landscape in the early part of the 2010s compared to the latter years. By the time Donald Trump had taken the oath of office, the nones had stopped switching to a different tradition entirely.

There are two central takeaways from this data for people of faith. The first is that religious switching has slowed considerably in the last few years. That's a double-edged sword for Christians looking to evangelize. The good news is that it appears that fewer nothing in particulars are becoming atheists or agnostics in recent years. However, that also means that fewer nothing in particulars are identifying as Protestants or Catholics on surveys, as well. But there's also a clear signal about how people of faith should think about the nones. If a Christian is trying to be strategic about reaching out to those without a religious affiliation, the data tells an unmistakable story: trying to convert atheists is going to end in failure ninety-nine times out of a hundred. The success rate for evangelizing agnostics is higher but still not great, succeeding just one in thirty times. However, that rate goes up dramatically for nothing in particulars. The data indicates that one in six of them will move back toward a Christian tradition over a four-year period.

When I conceptualize what American religion looks like, I think a simple continuum can be very helpful without being overly reductive.

Figure 4.22. The religious continuum in the United States.

Data from Stephen Ansolabehere, Brian F. Schaffner, and Sam Luks, Cooperative Congressional Election Study, Cambridge, MA: Harvard University, http://cces.gov. harvard.edu.

Atheists occupy the far left of the landscape in figure 4.22 and make up about 7 percent of the American population. The data indicates that they are almost completely dismissive of religion. Nine in ten never attend church and 95 percent say that religion is "not at all important." They are the hardest to convert.

Just to the right of atheists are agnostics, who also make up 6 percent of Americans. They are still fairly averse to religious behaviors and beliefs. For instance, seven in ten of them never attend church, and the same share say that the religion is "not at all important." Many of them become atheists over a nine-year period, but a slightly larger number become nothing in particulars as well. They are somewhat more likely to become Christians than atheists but the probability of conversion is very low.

However, the next group over is the nothing in particulars, which appears to be somewhat of a transfer station between religious groups on one side and atheists and agnostics on the other side. They are clearly warmer and more welcoming to religion than atheists and agnostics, but half of them never attend church services. Yet where they end up over a nine-year period is much more diverse and equally distributed. While 10 percent become agnostics and 6 percent become atheists, another 8 percent move into a non-Christian faith tradition, and 15 percent affiliate with a Christian tradition. For those 13 percent who move from nothing in particular to atheist or agnostic, the likelihood of them ever joining a Christian tradition is remote. If one wants to identify the harvest for new religious converts, it can be found among the one in five Americans who say that they are nothing in particular.

CONCLUSION

While it still seems useful to refer to atheists, agnostics, and nothing in particulars as religious nones, I hope this chapter serves as a word of caution to anyone who tries to paint this group with a broad brush. Atheists are some of the most educated individuals in the United States, and many of them have above-average incomes. They are also very male dominated. They describe themselves as liberals and often vote for Democratic candidates. They are incredibly politically active, engaging in behaviors of all types to help their preferred candidates and advocate for their policy positions. They are also far from organized religion and are incredibly unlikely to become Christians.

It seems that agnostics are a somewhat more restrained version of atheists. They too have high levels of education and enjoy high incomes. They are slightly less liberal than their atheist counterparts but also lean toward the Democrat side of the political spectrum. They engage in politics a great deal more than the average American but somewhat less than atheists. They do participate in church activities more than atheists but not very often, and very few of them are open to a Christian message.

Nothing in particulars are the largest group and share little in common with atheists or agnostics. While their gender distribution reflects that of the United States as a whole, they have incredibly low levels of educational attainment, and many of them make below-average incomes. Socially and politically, they are isolated. They don't attend rallies, they don't go to political meetings, and they don't put up political yard signs. However, they are not as far from religion as atheists or agnostics. A minority of them attend church at least once a month, and just four in ten say that religion is "not at all important" to them. About one in six of them becomes affiliated with a Christian tradition over a four-year period.

However, nothing in particulars represent the fastest-growing religious group in the United States today. Their numbers have increased a full six percentage points in just the past decade. The group also seems by and large to be struggling in American society. About six in ten of them are making less than $50,000 per year. They seem isolated as well. These are the people who may be the most receptive to faith and the most likely to gain real social and economic benefits from being part of a religious community. If religious groups want to reverse the growth of the nones, they should look no further than the nothing in particulars in their midst.

CHAPTER 5

Pandemic: Punctuated Equilibrium or Business as Usual?

On April 12, 2020, the Christian world celebrated Easter Sunday, a reminder to followers of Jesus Christ that He rose from the dead after He had been crucified three days prior. Easter is supposed to be one of the most hopeful days in the world for those who are Christians. Easter 2020 was unlike any other in the history of the United States, however, because almost no one was in a church pew that Sunday morning to be reminded of the possibilities and promises of the resurrection.

I remember rising early that Easter morning and driving the few minutes to the church. The cross that has sat above the altar for six decades was not draped with the traditional purple cloth; the Easter lilies were not spread out across the platform. The halls were not filled with women wearing their Easter dresses and men wearing suits and ties. Instead, the building was completely empty. I walked into the auditorium and sat in the back pew (I am a Baptist, after all), read a few chapters from scripture, and said a short prayer. Then, I left. It's an experience I won't ever forget—an empty church on Easter.

Just a few weeks prior, the United States government had declared a state of emergency in response to the rapid spread of the novel coronavirus across the United States. As a result of hospitals becoming overwhelmed with COVID-19 patients, governors across the

United States signed executive orders which forced all nonessential workers to shelter in place. The goal of those lockdowns was to control the spread of a virus that was potentially deadly and had no highly effective treatment. Because of these directives, almost all houses of worship had suspended gathering in person by Easter Sunday in 2020. So, what is usually one of the high points of the Christian calendar, where Christians don their Sunday best and pose for family pictures, was replaced with households huddled around computer screens in their pajamas, watching while their pastor preached from his or her home office.

Looking back on that moment now, with over two years of perspective, it's hard to recall just how much fear and uncertainty the average person was feeling during those first harrowing weeks of the COVID-19 pandemic. No one was sure how the virus was transmitted, and no public health officials could provide any real estimate of its mortality rate. So, the most prudent path was the most cautious one. Schools, businesses, and churches went into lockdown and hoped that medical science would come through.

But beyond the anxiety and isolation that COVID-19 brought to hundreds of millions of people across the world, the lockdowns also represented a grand social experiment we have not seen in our lifetime: the United States, for all practical purposes, shut down for at least a few weeks. People who had gone to church every weekend for decades now had to figure out a new Sunday morning routine. Then, a few weeks or a few months later, some churches began to let people back into the pews. Many congregations required masking and distancing, while others threw caution to the wind and began to worship like the coronavirus had never been discovered.

The Pew Research Center fielded a poll the first week of March 2021, and even after nearly a full year of pandemic restrictions, huge shares of American houses of worship were still utilizing procedures to mitigate the spread of the virus. Among those who said that they attended church (either virtually or in person) in the prior month, just 12 percent of respondents said that their church was operating in the same manner as it did before the COVID-19 outbreak. Another

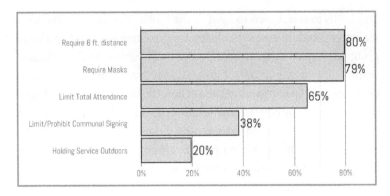

Figure 5.1. Actions taken by your church due to COVID-19.

Pew Research Center, American Trends Panel Wave 84. March 2021. https://tinyurl.com/5dfvyy2d

18 percent said that their house of worship was not open to the public for in-person worship, and 64 percent said that their church had adopted at least some precautions.

For those who indicated that their house of worship was still employing COVID-19 mitigation policies, masking and social distancing were clearly the most popular choices at about 80 percent of churches. In addition to those approaches to slowing the spread, two-thirds of churches that were meeting face to face put limits on the number of attendees. Nearly 40 percent said that their church had limited or prohibited communal singing, and one in five were only meeting outdoors. The data tells a clear picture: very few houses of worship were meeting without restrictions in March of 2021, and many churches had adopted most of the CDC guidelines when it came to slowing the spread of the virus.

As social scientists, we are always on the lookout for "natural experiments." These are events that happen outside the friendly confines of a lab on a college campus. In contrast, a natural experiment is an event that forces a large number of people to change their behavior in a clear, abrupt, and disruptive way. A famous example of this is the draft that the United States military used in the 1960s and 1970s to select men to fight in the war in Vietnam. It was done via lottery, and thus was the closest we can come to exposing a large group of people to a treatment (in this case, fighting in the military) while also creating a control group (those not drafted). There have been dozens of papers written about how those who got drafted have different levels of educational attainment, household income, and political views compared to those who did not fight in the conflict in Southeast Asia. It was obviously a life-altering experience for tens of thousands of men born in the 1940s and 1950s, but it also afforded social science a tremendous opportunity to understand the long-term impacts of serving in a combat zone.

Needless to say, academics have not been able to replicate the natural experiment of the Vietnam draft lottery in the last five decades and for good reason. One of the most frustrating processes that a social scientist has to navigate is getting research approved by an institutional review board (IRB). The purpose of an IRB is to review a scholar's research plan to ensure that it meets the university's guidelines for ethical behavior and does not cause harm (physical or otherwise) to participants. Obviously, randomly selecting young people to go fight a war in a country on the other side of the globe would have not survived the IRB process.

In a similar way, I can only imagine how the IRB at Eastern Illinois University would have responded if I proposed a study in which the government forced tens of millions of Americans to stay away from their church for a month. But that's exactly what happened across the United States in March and April of 2020. While COVID-19 was a harrowing experience for all of us, it also meant that social science was handed a once-in-a-generation natural experiment to understand what happens when people fall out of the habit of religious attendance.

It's become obvious to me that even casual observers of American religion have a unique interest in this topic. It may be the question I get asked the most in interviews—what did COVID-19 do to American religion? This chapter is my attempt to answer that question with all the data sources I have available to me. In the following pages I will take you on a deep dive into what polling data tells us about how religious affiliation, church attendance, and religious belief shifted between 2019 and late 2021. Additionally, I will try to explain why in chapter 1, I only visualized graphs from the General Social Survey (GSS) through 2018, even though the GSS did another data collection effort in 2021.

If you are looking for an easy and straightforward answer to these questions, I must admit up front: you won't find it here. Instead, I hope you finish this chapter understanding just how difficult a seemingly simple question can be.

RELIGIOUS BELONGING

As I mentioned back in chapter 1, the General Social Survey (GSS) is the gold standard when it comes to the changes in religious demography over the last five decades. A big reason why it's so well respected among the scholarly community is its consistency. The GSS prides itself on asking its core questions in the exact same way with the exact same response options in each wave since its inception. That's tremendously valuable for those who study long-term trends because it means that when a certain group gets five percent bigger or five percent smaller, we know that it's not because the survey question or methodology changed. It has to be something else going on with society.

However, the global pandemic threw a serious curveball to the team at the National Opinion Research Council (NORC), which is charged with administering the GSS. The General Social Survey has always been collected in a face-to-face format. That's the way the very first survey was conducted back in 1972, and to maintain consistency, the team at the NORC stuck to that process for the next four decades. And, to be clear, that's a very hard way to administer surveys. It's incredibly expensive and time consuming to interview 2,500 Americans from all across the country for forty-five minutes each. But then, COVID-19 swept across the United States, and it became imprudent for the GSS to be collected via thousands of face-to-face surveys in the midst of a global pandemic. The team at the NORC huddled remotely and decided to move the survey to an online format, much like what is used at many other polling firms like the Pew Research Center and Cooperative Election Study.

The data for the 2021 GSS was collected from December of 2020 through May of 2021, and the team made it publicly available for analysis in November. It was a moment I had been anticipating for years—it was the equivalent of data nerd Christmas morning for me. I clicked the download button and patiently waited while the large data file was transferred to my hard drive. I had all my scripts ready to sort people into the seven religious traditions discussed previously and I made my first graph. My heart sank. Something was off.

Figure 5.2 visualizes the share of Americans who said that they had no religious affiliation in every year of the General Social Survey (GSS) from 1972 through 2021. Do you notice something that seems different about the data point in 2021? It's much, much higher than

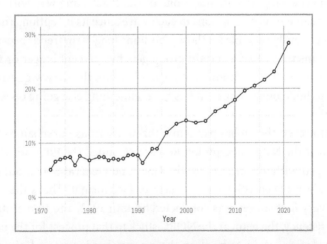

Figure 5.2. Share of nones in the General Social Survey, 1972–2021.

Data from the General Social Survey, a project of the independent research organization NORC at the University of Chicago, with principal funding from the National Science Foundation, https://gss.norc.org/Get-The-Data.

any trend line would predict. For reference, between 2006 and 2018, the total number of nones had risen from 16 percent to 23 percent. That averages out to just over a half a percentage point increase every year during that twelve-year time period. If the trend holds, we should expect the size of the nones to rise about two percentage points, give or take. Between 2018 and 2021, the GSS reported that the share of nones rose from 23 percent to over 28 percent. More than 5 percentage points in just three years—triple the rate that one would have expected. Something had clearly happened with the data, and I was on a frantic search to determine exactly what else had changed.

Religious demography is, and always will be, a zero-sum game. If one category grows larger, then another has to get smaller. Thus,

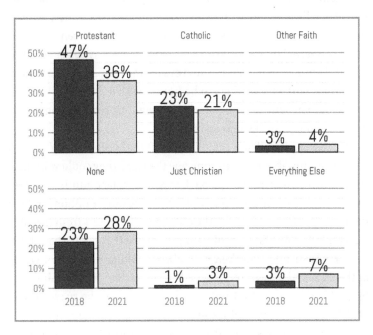

Figure 5.3. Size of religious traditions in 2018 vs. 2021.

Data from the General Social Survey, a project of the independent research organization NORC at the University of Chicago, with principal funding from the National Science Foundation, https://gss.norc.org/Get-The-Data.

if the nones grew over five percentage points in just three years, that share had to come from some other group. Figure 5.3 displays just how much shifting occurred between 2018 and 2021 using the broadest religious categories available. The most obvious movement is among Protestants who dropped eleven points in just three years. For someone who looks at survey data about religion on a near-daily basis, that presents a clear red flag. The size of religious groups typically changes very slowly over a period of decades, not years. Thus, there's more than ample reason to be skeptical of a big shift like this.

The most likely culprit for this shift is something that was touched upon in chapter 2, when the topic of discussion was social desirability bias. Recall that this is the idea that when a survey respondent is asked about something controversial like drug use, sexual behavior, or religiosity, they are going to give the answer that they think is the more socially acceptable one, not a response that accurately reflects their behavior. There are factors, however, that have been shown to drive down social desirability bias. One surefire way to get closer to truthful answers is to conduct surveys online instead of face to face. People are much more likely to be honest with a computer browser than a human being. If you don't believe me, just read the comments on anonymous online message boards.

Recall the conundrum that the team at the NORC was faced with when thinking about how to continue the GSS. They could wait until the pandemic abated, then go back to a face-to-face administration. Or, they could pivot to online. They chose the online option, and the data in figures 5.2 and 5.3 are the outcome. The results from the 2021 GSS provide some fairly compelling evidence that people have been less than truthful about their real religious affiliation in prior waves of the GSS, and that's likely due (at least in part) to social desirability bias. This data from 2021 bolsters the theory that the survey mode of delivery may have had a significant impact on the results from the GSS for the past several decades. In other words, there may have been more nones in the United States ten, twenty, or thirty years ago. They were just afraid to tell a survey administrator that they had no religious affiliation.

There may be something else going on worth considering as well. Those delivering the survey for the GSS have always been allowed to help respondents on questions that they didn't fully understand. There's obviously a fine line when it comes to nudging respondents toward an answer they wouldn't typically give versus just trying to categorize themselves correctly. For instance, if someone was asked about their current religion and they said, "Baptist" in a face-to-face situation, the administrator would have marked them as Protestant. But, if a Baptist was taking the survey online and didn't know what a Protestant was, they may not have been able to mark the correct box in the web browser and were essentially miscounted.

The lack of assistance by survey administrators has led to data from 2021 that is downright nonsensical in places. For those who described themselves as Protestant, the GSS asks a follow-up question to determine if they are Presbyterian, Episcopalian, or some other denomination. In 2018, 10 percent of all Protestants said that they were Southern Baptists. In 2021, that dropped to 2 percent. The share of United Methodists dropped from 7 percent to 2 percent at the same time. As this book has made clear, the share of people who are Christians is declining rapidly, but for the United Methodists and Southern Baptists to go from 17 percent of Protestants in 2018 to just 4 percent in 2021 is not feasible. While denominational respondents seem to disappear from the GSS in 2021, the share of Protestants who said that they were nondenominational rose by 10 percentage points in just three years. There's something more going on than social desirability bias. Instead, I would argue that because religious literacy is relatively low in the United States, many Americans were not able to classify themselves properly without the help of a survey administrator.

Thus, the reasons for not displaying the 2021 numbers in chapter 1 come into clearer view: they deviate so significantly from established trend lines that it's hard to believe that they accurately reflect the changes from American religion. However, all is not lost. Other surveys like the Cooperative Election Study (CES) did not need to change their delivery method because they have always been administered in

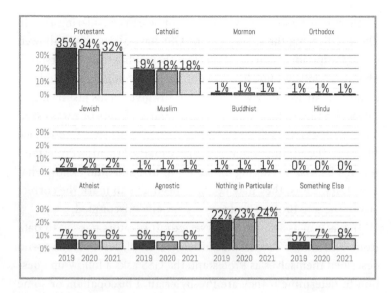

Figure 5.4. Size of religious groups, 2019–2021.

Data from Stephen Ansolabehere, Brian F. Schaffner, and Sam Luks, Cooperative Congressional Election Study, Cambridge, MA: Harvard University, http://cces.gov. harvard.edu.

an online format. To see if the large swings that were evident in the GSS carried over to the CES, I calculated the share of each religious group in 2019, 2020, and 2021. The results are visualized in figure 5.4.

As can quickly be gleaned, there's a lot more stability in these percentages compared to those from the GSS. The share of Americans who identified as Protestant declined about three percentage points between 2019 and 2021, which is right in line with the long-term trends. The share of Catholics dropped by a single percentage point in three years. Again, no reason for alarm there. In terms of other religious groups, there was almost no change in their share before or during the COVID-19 pandemic. For Latter-day Saints, Buddhists, Muslims, Jews, Hindus, and Orthodox Christians the share in the sample did not shift in a statistically significant way between 2019 and 2021.

When it comes to the nones, there are also very few noteworthy changes. The share of atheists dropped by .2 percent, which is not statistically or substantively significant. That exact same shift was evident among agnostics as well, one fifth of one percentage point. On the other hand, the share of Americans who identified as nothing in particular was 22 percent in 2019 and rose to 24 percent in the fall of 2021. Thus, the overall net gain for the nones was about two percentage points between 2019 and 2021. Again, that's right in line with the expected trend lines in the data that were evident long before the COVID-19 pandemic changed American society forever.

However, there's one more data source that could provide insights that are not available through the Cooperative Election Study or the General Social Survey. I've previously mentioned the Nationscape survey administered by the Democracy Fund, which is based at the University of California at Los Angeles, but it's worth returning to this instrument when discussing what happened to American religion during the pandemic. Here's why: instead of being collected annually, the Nationscape survey was fielded nearly every week from the middle of July 2019 through January of 2021. Said another way, there's a weekly survey fielded right through the heart of the pandemic. The average weekly sample for Nationscape was nearly 6,200 respondents, which is astronomically large and yields a total survey of 477,255 individuals. Thus with this tremendous data source we can track weekly changes in religious affiliation, which is visualized in figure 5.5.

I calculated the share of atheists, agnostics, or nothing in particulars each week throughout the 77-week collection period of Nationscape. I also combined all three groups and determined the overall size of the nones from the middle of July 2019 through the first few weeks of 2021. What should jump off the page is just how little movement there is, either way, in this data. In fact, the trend lines for both atheists and agnostics are nearly flat. In no week was the share of atheists higher than 5 percent or lower than 3 percent. For agnostics, the percentage never dropped below 4 percent or rose above 6 percent. And looking at the long-term linear trend, there's weak evidence that the share of atheists or agnostics actually may have dropped very slightly between 2019 and 2021.

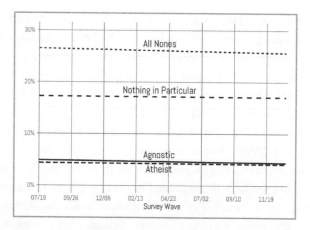

Figure 5.5. Share of nones measured weekly from July 2019 through January 2021.

Data from Tausanovitch, Chris and Lynn Vavreck. 2021. Democracy Fund + UCLA Nationscape Project, October 10-17, 2019 (version 20211215). https://www. voterstudygroup.org/nationscape

For nothing in particulars, that same general trend emerges as well. However, the overall percentages are obviously much larger. The share of nothing in particulars was never lower than 15 percent and did not rise above 19 percent in any week that survey data was collected. In terms of the overall trend line, there's almost nothing noteworthy to report. The share of nothing in particulars did not shift in a substantively significant way from the Summer of 2019 through Christmas of 2020, when a significant wave of the COVID-19 pandemic was hospitalizing tens of thousands of Americans. When the three groups are combined, the share of Americans who were nones hovered around 26 percent across the entire sampling period. Again, if there is any trend line to speak of, it's a downward one. According to this very large data source from Nationscape, the share of nones may have actually dropped by a percentage point during the first year of the global pandemic. There's certainly no clear evidence in the Cooperative Election Study or the Nationscape survey that points to a dramatic rise of the nones due to the global pandemic.

RELIGIOUS BEHAVIOR

When it comes to the three dimensions of religiosity (behavior, belief, and belonging), there's ample reason to assume that religious behavior would see the most appreciable drop due to the COVID-19 lockdowns. With tens of thousands of houses of worship closing their doors across the United States in the spring of 2020, there was just no outlet for people to attend religious services. Even after some of them began to allow parishioners back in the pews, they often required church goers to reserve spots ahead of time, wear

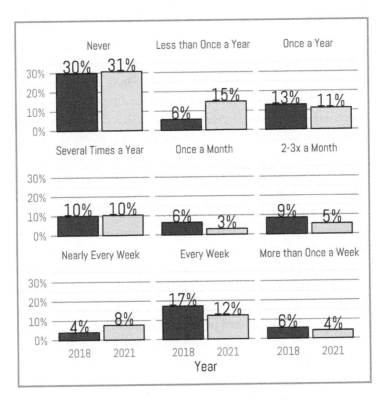

Figure 5.6. Change in church attendance, 2018 vs. 2021.

Data from the General Social Survey, a project of the independent research organization NORC at the University of Chicago, with principal funding from the National Science Foundation, https://gss.norc.org/Get-The-Data.

masks, and maintain physical distance. For older parishioners who were more concerned with the possibility of catching COVID-19, there was a greater reluctance to return to worship. Given all these obstacles to returning to church, it would come as no surprise if worship attendance numbers dropped significantly during the course of the pandemic.

To begin with this line of inquiry, I analyzed the attendance question from the General Social Survey (GSS) in 2018 and 2021. It simply asks, "How often do you attend religious services?" Recall that the GSS prides itself on consistency, and therefore they did not alter the question text to include watching services online, nor did they include any mention of the global pandemic in their question. In addition, the response options didn't change between waves of the GSS.

There are some categories that shifted noticeably between 2018 and 2021, and there are some that barely budged. For instance, the share of Americans who said that they never attended services was 30 percent in 2018 and 31 percent in 2021. That does not represent a statistically significant change. However, one category that did go up is "less than once a year." Just 6 percent of respondents chose that option in 2018. That more than doubled in 2021 to 15 percent. Taken together, about 36 percent of Americans attended less than yearly in 2018, and the figure rose to 46 percent by 2021.

There was also some movement at the other end of the scale. For instance, the share who described their attendance as every week went from 17 percent to 12 percent between 2018 and 2021. Additionally, the percentage who attended more than once per week dipped slightly as well. But those who said their attendance was "nearly every week" doubled from 4 percent to 8 percent between 2018 and 2021. The share who attended nearly every week or more in 2018 was 27 percent. Three years later it had declined to 24 percent. A noticeable change, surely. But not a seismic shift in the number of people in church each week. It's also impossible to know if the share of people who chose "nearly every week" did so as a way of telling the survey administrators that they would have attended weekly in a typical year, even though the COVID-19 shutdowns made that impossible.

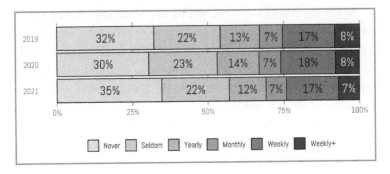

Figure 5.7. Religious service attendance, 2019–2021.

Data from Stephen Ansolabehere, Brian F. Schaffner, and Sam Luks, Cooperative Congressional Election Study, Cambridge, MA: Harvard University, http://cces.gov. harvard.edu.

It's always helpful to see if findings in one survey are replicated in another survey taken at roughly the same time. Fortunately, the Cooperative Election Study (CES) was also asking questions about religious service attendance in the fall of 2019, 2020, and 2021. The question prompt was, "Aside from weddings and funerals, how often do you attend religious services?" and again, there was no language added about attending services online during the global pandemic. The same six response options were provided in each wave of the CES and ranged from "never" to "more than once a week."

In figure 5.7 the distribution of responses for 2019–2021 are visualized and the clearest interpretation of the data is that very little changed during the COVID-19 lockdowns. In 2019, 32 percent of respondents reported never attending services. Another 22 percent described their attendance level as "seldom." Taken together, 54 percent of Americans were attending less than once a year before the coronavirus was discovered. Two years later the "never" or "seldom" attenders had risen three percentage points to 57 percent. While the size of that change is statistically significant, from a social science standpoint it's impossible to determine how much of this shift is related to COVID-19 and how much is just a continuation of trends that have been ongoing for decades.

At the top end of the scale, weekly or greater attendance was 25 percent in 2019 and it was 24 percent two years later. This shift is not statistically significant. In fact, the size of each category of religious attendance changed very little between 2019 and 2021. In only one case was the shift more than two percentage points—the never attenders in 2019 versus 2021.

For those who don't look at survey data regularly, this kind of result often comes with a bit of a shock. Almost all churches were closed down at some point during 2020, and many closed their doors again in late 2021 as another surge of the coronavirus sickened tens of millions of Americans. How can it be that church attendance didn't change in a significant way during this upheaval?

The answer lies in the differences between how the average American thinks about survey questions and how social science thinks about survey questions. Many people seem to think that those taking surveys expend a lot more time and energy answering these questions than they actually do. When asked about church attendance, some make the assumption that the person taking the survey does a mental tally of how often they went to services recently and then marks the appropriate box. But that's not how this process typically works. Instead, when posed this type of question, people's responses are not based on their actual behavior; instead, they think of the type of person they are and use that to guide their answers.

Here's an exercise to illustrate that. Imagine a woman in her late sixties named Helen. Helen was born and raised a United Methodist. She has been going to church every week for nearly her entire life except when she's gone on vacation or feeling ill. In 2018, she had a rough bout with the flu and took a longer than expected vacation to Florida. In total she missed about twenty weeks of church. However, when she answered a survey question about church attendance in late 2018, she indicated that she attends church weekly. She does so because she sees herself as the kind of person who is a faithful attender, except when something impedes her ability to go to church.

Is Helen lying when she answers that she attends weekly? Technically, yes. Her actual level of church attendance solidly fits in the "monthly" category. But Helen doesn't see herself that way. She sees herself as a weekly attender. And, from a social science perspective, I am fine classifying Helen as a more regular church attender because that's how she wants to present herself.

Or how about Helen's grandson, Chad. Chad is an avowed atheist who stopped believing in God when he was a teenager. Yet Chad and Helen have a very good relationship. When Helen had hip replacement surgery a few years ago, she asked Chad to drive her to church a few times during her recovery. He did so, and he sat beside her in the pew because he knew how important it was to his grandmother. When Chad was asked about church attendance on a survey, he said that he never attended services, when in actuality his attendance was either "seldom" or maybe even "yearly." Is Chad misleading survey administrators when he says he never attends church? I don't think he is. Instead, he is telling us that under normal circumstances he would never darken the church's door.

If we apply the same logic to the COVID-19 shutdowns, it becomes much more apparent why survey responses don't look that much different between 2019 and 2021. When someone like Helen was asked about her church attendance in November of 2020, she responded that she was a weekly attender even though her Methodist Church suspended services for several months during the worst parts of the pandemic. Helen didn't do a mental tally of her actual church attendance. Instead, she gave an answer that reflected how she saw herself: as a weekly attender.

RELIGIOUS BELIEF

There's another way to consider the impact that COVID-19 had on religiosity, and that's belief. The General Social Survey began asking respondents what they believed about God in 1988. Respondents are given six options ranging from "I don't believe in God" to "I

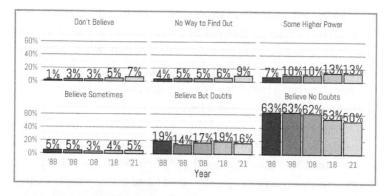

Figure 5.8. Change in religious belief, 1988–2021.

Data from the General Social Survey, a project of the independent research organization NORC at the University of Chicago, with principal funding from the National Science Foundation, https://gss.norc.org/Get-The-Data.

know God really exists and I have no doubts about it." It's possible that the global pandemic was just the event to drive people to more deeply consider their spiritual health and their relationship to God. In the first weeks of the lockdown, the *Wall Street Journal* published an op-ed from Robert Nicholson titled "A Coronavirus Great Awakening?" in which he pondered the possibilities that the forced isolation of COVID-19 would lead many Americans to come into a deeper relationship with God. He asked, "Will Americans, shaken by the reality of a risky universe, rediscover the God who proclaimed himself sovereign over every catastrophe?" The data doesn't seem to indicate that this was the case.

I calculated responses to the belief in God question in 1988, 1998, 2008, 2018, and 2021 to provide a sense of trajectory. Those results are displayed in figure 5.8. The share of Americans who said that God doesn't exist was just 1 percent in 1988. That had risen to 5 percent in 2018 and then creeped up two percentage points by 2021. There was also a noticeable rise in the portion of Americans who took an agnostic view of God from 6 percent to 9 percent between 2018 and 2021. All told, the share of Americans who had an atheist or agnostic belief in God was 12 percent before the pandemic and 15 percent in 2021. That difference was not statistically significant.

The middle part of the belief spectrum saw almost no movement over the last few years. Those who believed in some Higher Power stayed the same, which was also the case among those who said, "I find myself believing in God some of the time, but not at others." The share that indicated they believed in God but still had some doubts dropped about three percentage points between 2018 and 2021. There was also a three-percentage-point drop in those that believed in God without a doubt, from 53 percent to 50 percent. Yet, it's prudent to point out that the share of Americans who did not doubt God's existence dropped only ten points between 1988 and 2008, but then fell nearly that same amount again between 2008 and 2018.

Looked at in its totality, the data on this question from the GSS does not point to the conclusion that COVID-19 led to a Great Awakening where tens of millions of Americans returned to a faith in God. In fact, the most honest interpretation of the data is that people continued to express more doubts and reservations about God's existence. But, again, it's hard to ascertain if the pandemic accelerated trends that have been going on for years or if the depression, isolation, and grief that millions of Americans felt in 2020 and 2021 pushed more of them away from a certain belief in God.

While the Cooperative Election Study (CES) doesn't ask many questions about religious belief, it does ask, "How important is religion in your life?" and provides four response options from "not at all important" to "very important." Obviously this question is not specific in terms of what type of religion one believes in or in a specific type of theology based on Jesus or Mohammed. However, its value may be in its vagueness. If someone were to have a spiritual awakening during COVID-19, it would likely show up using this question. To get a sense of how responses to that question have trended, I've included results from 2008 through 2021 and visualized them in figure 5.9.

In 2008, fourteen percent of respondents said religion was not important at all and nearly the same share said it was not too

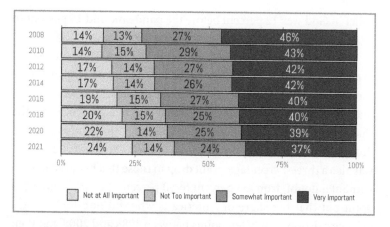

Figure 5.9. Importance of religion, 2008–2021.

Data from Stephen Ansolabehere, Brian F. Schaffner, and Sam Luks, Cooperative Congressional Election Study, Cambridge, MA: Harvard University, http://cces.gov. harvard.edu.

important in their lives. That left nearly three quarters who indicated that religion was at least somewhat important to them in 2008. But, from that point forward there's a slow and steady trend away from religiosity. By 2018, the share who said religion was "not at all" or "not too important" had risen to 35 percent, an increase of eight percentage points over a decade. But, notice how slow and steady the trend lines move for these categories. From 2010 through 2021, the share who said that religion was very important to them never declined by more than two percentage points from wave to wave. This is strong evidence of how public opinion moves gradually over a long period of time. One or two percentage points is essentially imperceptible over a year or two. But, when those percentages begin to pile up, a ten-to-fifteen-point shift over a decade is clearly felt by the average American.

However, it would be quite an empirical leap to say that Americans, on the whole, saw a wholesale return to faith—or, indeed, the opposite—during the COVID-19 pandemic. Because the CES is conducted in the fall, both the 2020 and 2021 surveys were collected at especially difficult points in the pandemic, as cases were ramping up and hospitals were filled to capacity. The fact is that the share who said religion is not at all important rose four points while the percentage who said religion was very important dropped by three points. That may be COVID-19 related, but if this graph was shown to someone who had no idea about the global pandemic, would those last two years look like outliers? I don't think that they would. Instead, these recent shifts are more likely continuations of a larger trend that dates back decades.

CONCLUSION

As all things are in social science, this is another clear example of why it's so hard to answer a seemingly simple question about what has happened and is currently happening in the world around us. It seems logical to assume that things should be different after the global pandemic. All of us, no matter our race, gender, income bracket, or religious affiliation had our lives disrupted in ways both big and small over the past several years. Many Americans fell out of the habit of doing things like going to church or eating in restaurants because they were no longer available. At the same time, some of us picked up new weekly rituals to replace those things that were lost. But all those little changes in behavior don't always add up to systemic changes in society that will register in large-scale surveys. Instead of being able to definitely say what has changed about American religion since 2019, we are left with a fairly fuzzy picture of the American religious landscape.

Looked at in its totality, the data seems to be telling us that not much has changed in terms of the trajectory of American religious belief, behavior, or belonging due to COVID-19. Fewer Americans are attaching themselves to a religious tradition, a smaller percentage are attending religious services on a regular basis, and a dwindling share say that they believe in God without any doubts. That was the case between 2016 and 2018 and that's surely the case between 2019 and 2021 as well.

However, I also think that it's reasonable to believe that the global pandemic may have sped up this secularization process just a bit, too. But not in the way that most people think. When I mention that to a friend or colleague, they typically respond by saying, "Oh, because people got out of the habit of going to church and just didn't go back?" While that may have happened for some people, I think the bigger impact of COVID-19, at least in the near term, is that it sped up generational replacement. For instance, the CDC's COVID-19 mortality tracker indicates that just over a million people died with the coronavirus listed as a potential cause on their death certificate between March of 2020 and the summer of 2022. Of those COVID-19 deaths, 75 percent of them were at least 65 years old. In the general population, less than 17 percent have seen their 65th birthday. While it's hard to estimate with tremendous precision, it's very likely that at least half a million older Americans died prematurely due to COVID-19.

Recall that back in chapter 3, I described how the Silent Generation was 72 percent Protestant and Catholic and 18 percent none. In comparison, Generation Z was 36 percent Protestant and Catholic and 48 percent none. One thing that we know about the novel coronavirus was that mortality was much higher among the oldest patients. That means a disproportionate number of the Silent Generation and the Baby Boomers succumbed to the virus, and they were replaced by thousands of members of Generation Z who came of age between 2019 and 2021. One of the grim implications of this reality is that America has become less religious not by any single person leaving faith or their church behind, but instead through simple generational replacement that was sped up due to COVID-19.

The more I struggle through this data, the more I am also confronted with another empirical reality: scholars of American religion won't be able to answer these types of questions definitively for another few years. We need to see if trends slow down in 2022 and 2023. If so, then we can clearly call 2020–2021 an outlier. There's not enough data to do that just yet. I am, however, hopeful about several academic projects that are focused on trying to answer these questions with greater specificity. The most prominent of these is the *Exploring the Pandemic Impact on Congregations* project, which is a five-year effort of scholars based at the Hartford Institute for Religion Research and funded by the Lilly Endowment. It's a multifaceted data collection effort using both quantitative surveys and qualitative techniques like interviews and focus groups to assess how the pandemic changed the lives of not only congregants but also clergy. These efforts, along with others, will allow the picture to become much clearer over the next few years.

There's a concept that I teach my students in public policy called punctuated equilibrium. It's borrowed from evolutionary biology, where it's described as the phenomenon when rapid change happens in a very short period of time followed by a long stretch of stagnation. The classic example of this is how much public policy changed in the wake of the terrorist attacks on September 11th, 2001. In just a few months, several major pieces of legislation moved through Congress including the passage of the USA PATRIOT Act and the creation of the Department of Homeland Security as well as the Transportation Security Administration. There have been fewer changes to domestic security in between 2002 and 2022 than occurred during the last three months of 2001. As Winston Churchill famously stated, "Never let a good crisis go to waste." That doesn't seem to be the case for American religion and the coronavirus.

For observers of American culture, many assumed it would serve as a moment of punctuated equilibrium. Many nones hoped it would be the nudge needed for millions of Americans who were on the fence to leave religion behind forever. At the other end of the religious spectrum, committed people of faith believed that COVID-19 could serve as a catalyst for religious revival. The data says that neither got their wish. There was no dramatic movement either toward or away from religiosity in the United States between 2019 and 2021. Instead, it was more business as usual. The nones continued to slowly rise.

CHAPTER 6

What We Can Change
and What We Cannot

One of the things that I try to do in the college political science classes I teach is to get my students to understand and think deeply about the big picture. Often, educators at all levels can get stuck in the rut of having students memorize esoteric facts that are quickly forgotten once the next exam is handed in. Giving them a view through a wider lens will provide them with a framework to process information for the rest of their lives. Having seen the value of big-picture thinking for my students, I invite you to take a deep dive with me as I conclude this book.

TWO UNSTOPPABLE FORCES

Globalization

I believe the most important force in American life today is globalization. Not a single person alive is immune to the effects of the increasingly globalized economy. Simply put, this is why most computers, automobile parts, and clothing are now made in the developing world. Capital is now mobile, and when the biggest expense a company faces is labor, business leaders naturally seek places where their products can be cheaply and effectively made. That is not in the United States.

Sensing that major manufacturers were on the lookout for places to build factories on a grand scale in the 1970s, countries primarily in Southeast Asia began to pour hundreds of billions of dollars into infrastructure, transportation, and technology, making access to cheap foreign labor even easier for Fortune 500 companies. Countries made these investments to transform their local economy, but the result has been to change the entire planet.

These shifts have sent shockwaves across the United States. In 1949, nearly one-third of all American adults worked in a factory. But by 2019, that number had dropped to just 8.5 percent.[1] In the wake of massive offshoring, America has often struggled to find its footing in the new globalized economy. One of the ramifications of this process has been wage stagnation for those in the middle class. According to the Pew Research Center, the peak of American earnings was in the early 1970s.[2] American workers are more productive than at any point in history, yet they have the same purchasing power they did four decades ago.

Almost every economist who studies globalization says that it would be nearly impossible to meaningfully reverse the offshoring of American manufacturing without spending millions of dollars that would never be recovered through jobs coming back to the United States. Trying to stop the flow of jobs out of the United States is the equivalent of trying to contain a forest fire that is engulfing millions of acres by bringing in larger fire hoses. No matter how much water is dumped on the flames, it will likely have very little impact on the outcome.

Not that the impossibility of the challenge has stopped politicians from trying, however. Candidates from both parties make the promise that they will make the bringing back of manufacturing jobs to the United States a central part of their platform. In February 2016, then presidential candidate Donald Trump made the offshoring of over two thousand jobs from a Carrier air-conditioning plant in Indiana a centerpiece of his stump speech. After being offered tens of millions of dollars in subsidies from the federal government to stay in the United States, Carrier agreed to keep about seven hundred jobs in Indiana. (Note that the company said it would use the government subsidies to invest in automation which will eventually lead to the elimination of even more positions.[3])

In addition to brokering these types of incentive packages for American manufacturers, Donald Trump also tried to combat globalization with tariffs. Early in his negotiations with Carrier, Trump threatened to institute a 35 percent tariff on any Carrier air conditioner imported into the United States. He levied tariffs on billions of dollars of goods flowing in from China as a means of pressuring that country into honoring prior trade agreements. These efforts to implement a protectionist economic policy have aimed to stem the tide of globalization, but by almost all accounts, they have been unsuccessful.

President Biden has also tried to use legislative avenues to impede the growth of globalization. For instance, in August 2022, he signed a bill that would include tax credits for electric vehicles but with several big caveats. One of those stipulations is that only vehicles that are assembled in North America would be eligible for tax credits—a small change that effectively disqualified half of the electric vehicles sold in the United States. But the most onerous change is that a significant percentage of minerals used in the batteries for these vehicles must come from countries that have a free-trade agreement with the United States. Industry experts report that it may be impossible to meet this benchmark as 90 percent of these materials are processed in China.[4] Trying to bring the manufacturing of electric cars to American shores is surely a laudable goal, but it may end up merely making it harder and more expensive to transition the American auto industry to an all-electric future.

Globalization has also led disaffected American workers to look for someone to blame for their economic misfortunes, and US leaders have been quick to find scapegoats. Donald Trump not only liked to blame the Chinese for the ills of the American working class but also continued to pin many of the problems of American society on undocumented immigrants to the United States. This has led to an increase in hate crimes against racial minorities and the construction of billions of dollars of fencing around the southern border.

That's not to say that politicians on the left have not found a place to direct their ire about wage stagnation as well. Senator Bernie Sanders ran two high-profile campaigns for president of the United States focusing on the issue. In his view, the reason that most Americans are not getting ahead is that rich and powerful business leaders in the United States are capturing billions of dollars in newly created wealth rather than sharing it with the average American. The solution for Sanders, and others on the left side of the political spectrum, is to heavily tax the richest Americans and provide more government services to the American populace.

The sad reality of human nature is that when things go wrong, we look for someone to blame. For those on the right, it's China and immigrants. For liberals, it's economic elites. But casting blame on any of these groups sidesteps the reality that globalization is only going to accelerate, and the problem facing American workers in a decade won't be foreigners taking their jobs or the concentration of wealth in the hands of a few, it will be automation. In short, no matter what any politician or business leader says, there is very little they can do to truly reverse the changes to American society brought about by technology and globalization.

Secularization

I think it's helpful for people of faith to think about the rise of the nones in much the same way as globalization. In both cases, the same cold, hard fact is true: we cannot stop it. Both waves are only continuing to build in strength and speed. Any efforts to impede them will be futile. To try to stop globalization by imposing tariffs on imported goods is the functional equivalent of attempts to stop secularization by posting the Ten Commandments in more American courthouses.

Globalization and secularization followed much the same course. The changes were gradual, happening so slowly that by the time many people realized the significance of the shift in American society, it was already too late. Millions of people born in the 1960s and 1970s were content to follow the life course their parents had. They assumed they would graduate from high school, go work in the factory, and live a good and fulfilling life. Then it all went up in smoke. When their jobs moved overseas, many of them were too old, or too set in their ways, to learn a new skill or accept the shifting reality. They fell through the cracks of the American economy—casualties of globalization. Government and business were unwilling or unable to reach out to them in effective ways to retrain them for this new reality.

In the same way, churches happily glided along during the 1950s and 1960s, spending massive amounts of time and money on programs and buildings. The pews were packed and offering plates were filled. Then in the early 1990s, the American religious landscape began a tectonic shift. Many prayed for a day when the young people who grew up in their churches would get married and return with their own children, but that never happened. Churches kept using the same old methods of evangelism and church growth. They bought LED signs and printed more tracts. They redoubled their efforts on "Invite a Friend" Sunday and put on more elaborate productions for Easter and Christmas. As the 1990s gave way to the new millennium, the pews got a little emptier and the collection plates a bit lighter. Many churches began using their endowment funds to make up for budget shortfalls. Now, a few decades later, many of them are closing up shop—casualties of secularization.

All these changes can seem so depressing. How do people of faith deal with some of the statistics presented in this book when they are left with the overwhelming fact that the America of tomorrow will look nothing like the America of thirty years ago? I am reminded of a conversation between two characters in the 2014 movie *Wish I Was Here*. Aidan, played by Zach Braff, is racked with grief that his father, Gabe, has had a reoccurrence of cancer.

Aidan exclaims, "There's so much bad news all at once. What do we do?"

And Gabe calmly responds, "What do you mean, 'What do we do?' We move forward. It's the only direction God gave us."

HOW DO WE MOVE FORWARD?

Reinhold Niebuhr succinctly captures the advice I would give the modern church about how to respond to the rise of the nones: "God, grant me the serenity to accept the things I cannot change, the courage to change the things I can, and the wisdom to know the difference."

Let me make one small amendment: "and the data to know the difference."

Let's begin with the things that cannot be changed. I think that no matter how effective the church was at evangelism or missions or community service over the past four decades, those efforts would have been only slightly effective at stopping the rise of the nones. The best apologists, the most charismatic speakers, or the catchiest praise and worship bands would not have held secularization at bay. There's no way to know for certain, but it's fair to say that a significant chunk of the increase in the unaffiliated was due to shifts in American culture away from religion. Recall that Max Weber believed that as educational levels increased, people would begin to look toward science, not God, to explain the world. It is foolhardy to think that what happened in Europe, which was also experiencing a dramatic rise in educational levels, would not, to some extent, come to American shores. The reality is simply this: Americans used to be Christians simply by default, not because of their belief in the words of the Apostles' Creed. Secularization merely gave permission for a lot of people to express who they truly are—religiously unaffiliated.

But I must make one more data-driven observation. While I have shared dozens of data points across these pages about the tremendous number of Americans who no longer affiliate with a religion, I have intentionally left out a crucial piece of information: religious belief in this country is still surprisingly robust. In 1988, 2 percent of respondents to the General Social Survey said that God didn't exist and another 4 percent said that God might exist but there's no way to find out. In 2018, just 7 percent of people said that there was no God, and 9 percent said there was no way to know for sure. While about 30 percent of Americans no longer affiliate with religion, just 16 percent of Americans do not believe God exists. The issue is not that interest in spiritual matters has declined; it's that people do not want to label themselves as a Christian, Mormon, or Buddhist.

So what gives? If almost all Americans still believe in the divine, we should not be seeing the number of nones continue to slowly and steadily grow every passing year. But we are. So how do we respond? To return to Niebuhr's prayer, it's crucial for the church to focus on what can be changed. I'll discuss two possible avenues for change. One is related to how we have not listened to the nones' stories, and the other to how Christians, specifically white Protestants and Catholics, have made Democrats feel more and more marginalized with every passing election.

Behind Every Survey Respondent Is a Story

One of the things I constantly have to remind myself when I do data analysis is that every single row on my spreadsheet represents a human being who has a story to tell. People who grew up in faith communities but left them when they moved into adulthood all have a story to tell. Some of those stories are not that enlightening. The church just didn't work for them, and they saw no benefit in regular attendance. Others left for reasons that are much more instructive. Whatever their motives, we should be seeking out people willing to tell their stories, inviting them to tell us, and listening—*really* listening—to them.

What sort of stories might we hear? Many people have been abused at the hands of people who claim to act in the name of Jesus Christ. For decades, parents have told their LGBT children that they are no longer allowed in their house. Some have been made to feel unwelcome when they've asked too many questions about why God acted so terribly in the Old Testament or how an all-powerful force could allow children to die of cancer. Others have been raised in such a controlling environment that rebellion has become their motivating force in adulthood. Because of some of the previously mentioned effects of globalization, many have been forced to work two or three jobs to make ends meet, and church is a luxury these people feel they can't afford. Some felt ostracized for marrying someone of a different faith or getting pregnant out of wedlock. These stories, and many more, are completely legitimate reasons to walk away from any institution—regardless of whether it embodies the Truth or not.

A phrase I often repeat to my students when we talk about respecting other people's political viewpoints is "Your world is not their world." I might also say, "Your story is not their story." I think many Christians have a hard time putting themselves in the shoes of the person who left church and never came back or those who never made the connection in the first place. They don't recognize that to belittle, minimize, or try to explain away the stories of those who walked away or never connected to a church home is to fail to understand that not everyone comes to faith the same way we did, and people do not stay (or leave, or stay away) for the same reasons we do either.

For those nones who have made it this far into this book—thank you. I am deeply appreciative that you are willing to listen to someone who is not from your social group try to describe it. It's always been my goal to objectively describe this incredibly important social movement. I hope that the prior chapters have done that, and that after looking at these dozens and dozens of graphs, you better understand where you place yourself in social, religious, and political space. One of the best things that we can do as social scientists is to let people know that they are not alone. As can be seen from this book, if you are a none, you are in very good company with tens of millions of people just like you across the United States.

But for those who describe themselves as "nothing in particular" when it comes to religion, I hope the data analyzed here serves as a warning. The portrait the data is painting is one in which this group of individuals is struggling—socially, financially, and politically.

Nothing in particulars are anti-institutional and distrustful of the world around them. Many of them, for very valid reasons, feel that American society has let them down. They are falling further behind as each year passes. It's completely understandable that this group of people wants to withdraw from a society that they believe is not looking out for them or their best interests. Withdrawing from all the vestiges of organized society is not the solution, however, to the problems of economic inequality and social isolation.

In 2022, a team of researchers published a study where they analyzed the Facebook friendships of seventy-four million Americans to determine what factors lead to economic mobility—the ability of someone born at the bottom of the economic spectrum to move into the middle or upper class as they progress throughout their life. What the researchers found was simple yet profound. Poor people who had a greater number of connections with rich people were much more likely to move up the economic ladder than those who had fewer connections.[5] And the data on the nones makes this point clear: nothing in particulars are some of the most economically disadvantaged people in American society, and they are also the least socially engaged. It's hard not to look at these statistics and conclude that by making these choices, nothing in particulars are making their financial situation worse.

Now, I know what some of you are thinking, "This pastor is trying to tell the nones to come back to church." But that's not what I am saying. Instead, I would strongly encourage the nones to become more socially involved in some way, shape, or form. That could mean joining the board at the local YMCA. Or volunteering at a fundraiser for the United Way. Becoming a member of the local Elks or Lions club is a great way to integrate into the local community. Making social connections and working for a worthwhile cause is a tremendous way to improve mental health but also possibly increase economic mobility. Checking out from American society may seem like an attractive option, but it only appears that way because the pervasiveness of social media has led many of us to believe that we are making meaningful social connections by liking and commenting on people's Facebook posts. Unfortunately, social media has only exacerbated our social and political polarization. We must actively work to rebuild relationships in the real world.

Beyond Every Survey Respondent Is Politics

That's not to say that there aren't ample reasons for why tens of millions of Americans reject religion entirely. It's impossible to look at the rise of the nones and not think that a significant cause of this shift in American society is politics. I know this observation has become an overwrought cliché, but God is not a Republican or a Democrat. That said, if someone walked into most Christian houses of worship this upcoming weekend, they would not find much evidence to support that conclusion. In 1972, half of all white weekly churchgoers were Democrats; now just a quarter are. Of the twenty largest predominantly white Protestant traditions in the United States, sixteen became more Republican between 2008 and 2018. Four in five white evangelical Protestants voted for Donald Trump for president in 2016. The totality of that shift is absolutely staggering, and for many people whose politics lean left but who still want to be part of a Christian community, there are no options for them locally. And some churches seem to go out of their way to make that reality known.

I'm friends with a number of pastors on Facebook, acquaintances I have picked up over the past fifteen years in ministry. Often, I feel like scrolling my newsfeed is a type of social science experiment. I'm just flabbergasted by how often these pastors post things that belittle, demean, or misrepresent the views of their political opposition. In my mind, what they are doing is no different from placing a sign on the front door of their church every Sunday morning that says, "No Democrats Allowed." If Christians want to seek and save the lost, why would some of them go out of their way to alienate a third of the population of the United States? There are already enough hurdles for someone who might want to come back to church. Why add another?

I have arrived at two conclusions about their words and deeds. The first is that these pastors don't realize there are Democrats who could potentially want to visit their church next Sunday. The second is that these pastors are convinced that no other political beliefs are compatible with the Gospel. And I see my liberal Christian friends fall into this trap as well. There are lots of people who voted for Donald Trump for well-considered reasons, and maligning these Republican voters does Christianity no favors. Either conclusion shows an unbelievable lack of awareness and leaves no doubt in my mind as to why so many people have become or remain religiously unaffiliated.

Now, that's not to say that all pastors engage in such behavior on social media. I know what many of those who are reading this may be thinking right now: *I don't preach politics on my Facebook feed or from the pulpit!* I agree with you, and so does the data.[6] Very few pastors are expressly political in their preaching. But pastors need to recognize that their members are absorbing political messages from other aspects of their church involvement. They might pick up clues from a conversation they had before church about property taxes or a Wednesday evening small-group discussion about abortion or gay marriage. There are no truly apolitical churches.[7]

I understand the conundrum that pastors face. Most of them realize that speaking about politics from the pulpit might engender support from a majority of congregants but drive others away, so they know it's prudent for them to steer clear. That's a natural response, and I think it comes from a good place. However, church members are always on the lookout for people to help them think about how to respond to current events or government policies. When pastors do not apply the Gospel to the very real concerns of modern society, they are opening the door for others to influence church members. Those "others" might be friends, family, pastors of other churches—almost anyone, really. But a pastor once mentioned to me that while he has a captive audience for one hour once a week, the cable news networks are piped into members' homes for eight hours a day, seven days a week. That's a sobering thought. If pastors don't give congregations guidance on how to think about politics, then they will get it from somewhere else. And unfortunately, what drives clicks, eyeballs, and ad revenue are media personalities who do their best to not only make their political party look good but make the other side of the aisle look ignorant, out of touch, and immoral.

So here's my suggestion: speak Truth to them. Preach sound biblical doctrine that cuts across the political spectrum. One of the theological principles that shapes the way I view the world dates back to the Old Testament. It's the concept of *imago Dei*—the understanding that every human being is created in the image and likeness of God, and because of that, every person on Earth is deserving of love and respect. It sounds so simple, yet it can have a profound impact on how we think, act, and vote.

The political implications of *imago Dei* are tremendous and should give pause to both Republicans and Democrats. This worldview rises above partisanship. It teaches that neglecting the poor is a violation of *imago Dei*, and it also teaches us that we should value the lives of the unborn. *Imago Dei* means that the disabled bear the image of the Creator, just like all of us. But *imago Dei* also teaches us that no matter someone's immigration status or the color of their skin, they were fearfully and wonderfully made. Those who follow *imago Dei* should fight for the concept of religious liberty not just for Christians but for all people of any faith tradition.

Think About the Horizontal

There's this saying in academia, "When you have a hammer, the whole world looks like a nail." It's often invoked by professors after they teach their students some new statistical method and it serves as a caution: "Just because I taught you this new technique doesn't mean it's the most appropriate one for the questions you are trying to answer." I distinctly remember the day that I really began to understand how linear regression worked. I ran home, booted up my laptop and started running dozens of models using every dataset I could get my hands on. Twenty-five-year-old me had a hammer, and I was ready to use it to build a new understanding of how religion and politics worked. After staring at that tiny screen for a couple of days I started to realize just how hard social science truly was and that understanding mathematical models was only a small part of the equation.

I think that's the trap that young pastors fall into, as well. They go to divinity school or seminary for a few years and go deep into the weeds of theology, church history, and the etymology of Hebrew and Greek words. By undergoing that level of study, a large part of seminarians' worldview is focused on the vertical dimension of religion—that is, the relationship that each human being has with God. Professors in divinity school talk about church growth in terms of the moving of the Holy Spirit, the spiritual health of the leadership team, and the ability of the preaching pastor to teach sound biblical doctrine from the pulpit. So, when pastors read this book and see dozens of graphs that visualize the decline of American religion, their knee-jerk reaction is to point to some type of spiritual failing of the church. They think that churches aren't preaching well enough, or they are watering down the Gospel—those are the solutions to the rise of the nones. Remember, if you have a hammer, the whole world looks like a nail. If you've been taught that all problems are spiritual ones, then the rise of secularism in the United States is going to be reversed through greater fidelity to the scriptures and the teaching of Jesus.

I was trained to think about the world in a different way. For social scientists, the solution to almost every problem that we face is in a careful analysis of the horizontal world—that is, how people relate to each other. When pastors think about a Sunday morning church service, they focus on the right songs being sung, the right scriptures being read, and the right sermon being preached. As a social scientist, I'm much more concerned with what happens in the ten or twenty minutes before the service starts and after it ends. That's when members of the congregation sit around and chat a bit. Those moments are when relationships are forged and connections are made. It's where single people in the church can find a potential spouse or young families can arrange a playdate for their children. It's a chance for people to just socialize with one another for a moment or two.

From my perspective, at the most basic level, churches are social organizations. They don't differ that much from the local Elks club or a slow pitch softball league. They are opportunities for people to meet up and work together for a common cause. And, in doing so, they have plenty of chances to make new friends or strengthen their bonds with people they have known for years. Yet, somehow, many churches seem to miss that simple reality: there are people in the pews who aren't there for the religious education or the polished worship team. They show up because it gives them a chance to find out what's happening in their local community or to see if they can arrange a time to meet up with their friends for dinner during the week. They just want to make connections. That's not to say that churches should downplay the fact that they are meeting to worship and draw closer to the Divine, but it's crucial to realize that thriving religious communities do both the vertical and horizontal well.

I've been asked by pastors dozens of times over the last two years how I would bring the nones back. The best answer I can give is, "Don't forget about the horizontal." Good preaching is important, but so is giving people space to just chat with each other. To that end, religious organizations need to create opportunities for relationships to forge and flourish. A monthly event that is completely social is a good place to start. A potluck meal with the congregation. A carnival in the church's yard with bounce houses and free food. A BBQ during the summer or a back-to-school event where school supplies are handed out. No pressure to end conversations early so that the pastor can preach an evangelistic sermon. No need to yell to each other as the worship band plays another chorus, when people are trying to carry on a conversation. Just an event that was created with the goal of allowing people to come together and meet their neighbors. In a post-COVID world, when tens of millions of Americans were forced to think about how much social connection means to them, churches would do a tremendous public service for their community by facilitating more social connection.

Will those events lead to more people in the pews on a Sunday morning? Probably not. But in my estimation, that should not be the only goal that religious organizations should focus on. As we discussed back in chapter 2, social capital is desperately needed in a rapidly polarizing society. People need opportunities to build bridges to other people in their neighborhood—to see them as human beings, not just random strangers. When that happens, it leads to all kinds of good outcomes: a greater willingness to volunteer to help other people in the community and an increased desire to see all of their neighbors flourish. Will that always lead to a new family joining the church? No, but it will lead to a community that is kinder, more gracious, and more generous. That sounds like the kind of place that people want to live, and for Christians that sounds like what the Kingdom of God is all about.

FEELING HOPELESS? JUST KEEP THROWING OUT SEED

If I were a younger man, this is the part of the book where I would try to offer some sage wisdom and practical advice to fill the pews back up. However, experience tells me that there is no easy answer. I became a senior pastor at the tender age of twenty-three. I had just started a graduate program and honestly needed to make some money to pay the rent. Luckily, the older congregants of a small church welcomed me with open arms. I thought that if I just preached really well and did a lot of visits, people would come to church. After a year, I left. I think that the church expected me to be a miracle worker, and I did nothing to downplay those expectations. I learned that just last year, the church officially closed its doors, and the building was razed a few weeks later.

The church I currently serve had fifty regular worshippers when I assumed the pulpit thirteen years ago. Today, we are down to about fifteen most Sundays. We've had weeks when the total attendance was in the single digits. Again, I thought that if I set myself on fire, people would come to watch me burn. That's not what happened. About five years into my ministry, I became listless and angry. Why wasn't the church growing? Why can't we bring in some young people? I thought of myself as a failure. I felt like one of those factory workers who got laid off after twenty years of hard work and dedication, wondering why my efforts weren't being rewarded.

I kept thinking about what the church used to be—nearly three hundred members with activities almost every day of the week and a tremendous influence on the community. Now we were struggling to keep the lights on. I was no different from the guys who meet for coffee at fast-food restaurants and talk about life before the factory closed. The word *nostalgia* can be translated "an ache for home." It seems that I, the coffee-shop crew, and frankly, a lot of people are consumed by this pining for a bygone era.

But after a period of wallowing, I realized that our church must move forward. So we stepped out in faith and began packing brown paper sacks filled with food for schoolchildren who were struggling with poverty in our community. We started with thirty bags per weekend. We had no idea if it would work or if we could actually afford it. Nearly a decade later, we pack nearly three hundred bags of food each weekend and serve three local schools. Every time we think that the money is going to run out, a check shows up. Like the factory worker who sees the plant closure as an opportunity to go back to school and retrain for a different career, our food program was the avenue we took to keep moving forward.

When we first started organizing our brown bag program, some members of the congregation thought that we should drop a tract into the bags, but I refused. For me, the purpose of those bags was not to try to bring people to Christ. It was to show those kids that someone they don't even know loves them and wants to help. So, we just include a simple note saying who we are and what we are doing. We make sure to let them know that if they need help, they can just give us a call.

Well, one Friday, the phone rang. It was a grandmother of one of the children who had received a bag. The temperature had begun to drop, and her grandson didn't have a warm coat. She asked for help. It just so happened that we were having a rummage sale that weekend and had a fellowship hall full of clothes. We invited her to come down and take whatever she needed. Just an hour later, she and her grandson stuffed two armloads of clothes into her trunk and drove away.

I have no idea if that young man or his grandmother will ever come to know Christ. But here's what I do know: they left our church that day knowing that they were born in the image and likeness of God and that people who they had never met cared deeply about them. When that young man is sitting around as an adult one day, talking about spiritual things, he might have some bad things to say about the church, but I hope that when he tells his story of faith, he at least makes mention of the one time when he needed help and a church came to his rescue. That young man's story of faith will be just a bit different because of what our little church did for him. But there are millions of people who can't say the same thing, because for them, church did not make their lives better. It just made them feel worse.

One of my favorite parables from the Gospel of Matthew involves a farmer who is trying to plant seed. Jesus notes that some of the seed falls on inhospitable soil and never takes root, while other seed manages to find fertile ground, takes root, and creates a bountiful harvest. I firmly believe that the church needs to stop trying to control where the seed lands. The winds of secularization and polarization are swirling like never before. Most of that seed is going to fall on rocky soil, never to reap a harvest. And it seems that there are fewer people to spread it every year. It's easy to give up hope. But we must recall the words of the apostle Paul to the church in Galatia: "So let us not grow weary in doing what is right, for we will reap at harvest time, if we do not give up" (Gal 6:9). Seed that expresses the love and grace and hope of Jesus Christ is never truly lost. Don't give up!

Notes

CHAPTER 1

1 Sarah Kaplan, "It's Official: The Definition of a Kilogram Has Changed," *Science Alert*, November 16, 2018, https://tinyurl.com/ycb2xvbo.

2 Stacey Vanek Smith, "The Santa Suit," NPR, December 20, 2017, https://tinyurl.com/y2pmzvth.

3 Christopher H. Achen and Larry M. Bartels, *Democracy for Realists: Why Elections Do Not Produce Responsive Government* (Princeton and Oxford: Princeton University Press, 2017), 266.

4 In fact, historian Thomas Kidd wrote two hundred pages on the concept for his 2019 book, *Who Is an Evangelical?* (New Haven, CT: Yale University Press).

5 Carol Pipes, "Southern Baptists see baptisms, giving rebound in 2021," *Baptist Press*, https://tinyurl.com/38r4yn9a.

6 Sarah Pulliam Bailey, "White Evangelicals Voted Overwhelmingly for Donald Trump, Exit Polls Show," *Washington Post*, November 9, 2016, https://tinyurl.com/qfx2394.

7 Mary Newton Stanard, *Colonial Virginia: Its People and Customs* (Philadelphia: Lippincott, 1917).

8 "Marriage Equality," United Church of Christ, https://tinyurl.com/y2ut3hzd.

9 Ryan P. Burge, *20 Myths About Religion and Politics in America*. "Myth 18 – Mainline Protestants are politically liberal" (Minneapolis, MN: Fortress Press, 2022).

10 Kenneth D. Wald, "The Puzzling Politics of American Jewry (ARDA Guiding Paper Series)," Association of Religion Data Archives at the Pennsylvania State University, https://tinyurl.com/yx9oo3os.

11 Jana Riess, "Mormon Growth Continues to Slow, Especially in the US," *Religion News Service*, April 13, 2018, https://tinyurl.com/y3qgeglg.

CHAPTER 2

1 Heather Pringle, "The Slow Birth of Agriculture," *Science* 282, no. 5393 (1998): 1446–47.

2 See Deuteronomy 11 for evidence of this among the Hebrews.

3 Max Weber, *From Max Weber: Essays in Sociology*, trans. and ed. H. H. Gerth and C. Wright Mills (New York: Oxford University Press, 1946), 129–36.

4 Karl Marx, "Introduction to a Contribution of the Critique of Hegel's Philosophy of Right," in *The Marx Engels Reader*, trans. T. B. Bottomore (New York: W. W. Norton, 1972), 12.

5 Naftali Bendavid, "Europe's Empty Churches Go on Sale," *Wall Street Journal*, January 2, 2015, https://tinyurl.com/hux7x7q.

6 Fenggang Yang, *Religion in China: Survival and Revival under Communist Rule* (New York: Oxford University Press, 2011).

7 Seymour M. Lipset and Stein Rokkan, eds., *Party Systems and Voter Alignments: Cross-National Perspectives*, vol. 7 (New York: Free Press, 1967).

8 Alexis de Tocqueville, *Democracy in America*, trans. Arthur Goldhammer (New York: Library of America, 2004), 343.

9 Kenneth D. Wald and Allison Calhoun-Brown, *Religion and Politics in the United States* (Lanham, MD: Rowman & Littlefield, 2014), 21.

10 Pippa Norris and Ronald Inglehart, *Sacred and Secular: Religion and Politics Worldwide*, 2nd edition (Cambridge University Press, 2011).

11 Kodai Kusano and Waleed Ahmad Jami, "Selected anomalies or overlooked variability? Modernization is associated with secularization in countries with high historical wealth but is associated with increasing religiosity in post-communist or Christian-minority countries," *Current Research in Ecological and Social Psychology*, 3, 100036 (2022).

12 Robert N. Bellah, "Civil Religion in America," *Daedalus* 96, no. 1 (1967): 1–21.

13 Sarah Pulliam Bailey, "Christianity Is Declining at a Rapid Pace, but Americans Still Hold Positive Views about Religion's Role in Society," *Washington Post*, November 15, 2019, https://tinyurl.com/y2h38smw.

14 C. Kirk Hadaway, Penny L. Marler, and Mark Chaves, "What the Polls Don't Show: A Closer Look at US Church Attendance," *American Sociological Review* 58, no. 6 (1993): 741–52.

15 Benjamin Knoll and Cammie Jo Bolin, *She Preached the Word: Women's Ordination in Modern America* (Oxford University Press, 2018).

16 Elisabeth Noelle-Neumann, "The Spiral of Silence: A Theory of Public Opinion," *Journal of Communication* 24, no. 2 (1974): 43–51.

17 Pablo Porten-Cheé and Christiane Eilders, "Spiral of Silence Online: How Online Communication Affects Opinion Climate Perception and Opinion Expression regarding the Climate Change Debate," *Studies in Communication Sciences* 15, no. 1 (2015): 143–50.

18 Sherice Gearhart and Weiwu Zhang, "'Was It Something I Said?' 'No, It Was Something You Posted!' A Study of the Spiral of Silence Theory in Social Media Contexts," *Cyberpsychology, Behavior, and Social Networking* 18, no. 4 (2015): 208–13.

19 Sarah Pulliam Bailey, "White Evangelicals Voted Overwhelmingly for Donald Trump, Exit Polls Show," *Washington Post*, November 9, 2016, https://tinyurl.com/qfx2394.

20 Ryan Burge (@Ryanburge), "I am kind of shocked by how little the vote choice of white Christians changed across the last three elections," Twitter, October 27, 2019, https://tinyurl.com/y2n6sg8t.

21 Ryan Burge, "Why Politics May Kill White Churches," Religion News Service, May 29, 2019, https://tinyurl.com/y5uoctwc.

22 Wald and Calhoun-Brown, *Religion and Politics*, chapter 8.

23 Randall Balmer, "The Real Origins of the Religious Right," *Politico Magazine*, May 27, 2014, https://tinyurl.com/y3x46nzj.

24 Kevin M. Kruse, *One Nation under God: How Corporate America Invented Christian America* (New York: Basic Books, 2015).

25 Ryan Burge, "Democratic Party Is at an Inflection Point When It Comes to Courting Religious Voters," Religion News Service, October 1, 2019, https://tinyurl.com/y5kk5zeu.

26 Michael Hout and Claude S. Fischer, "Why More Americans Have No Religious Preference: Politics and Generations," *American Sociological Review* 67, no. 2 (2002): 165–90.

27 Michele F. Margolis, *From Politics to the Pews: How Partisanship and the Political Environment Shape Religious Identity* (University of Chicago Press, 2018).

28 Paul Djupe, Jacob R. Neiheisel, and Anand E. Sokhey, "Reconsidering the Role of Politics in Leaving Religion—The Importance of Affiliation," *American Journal of Political Science* 62, no. 1 (2018): 161–75.

29 Daniel A. Cox, The State of American Friendship: Change, Challenges, and Loss. Survey Center on American Life. https://www.americansurveycenter.org/research/the-state-of-american-friendship-change-challenges-and-loss/. June 8, 2021.

30 Gretchen Livingston, On Average, Older Adults Spend Over Half Their Waking Hours Alone. Pew Research Center. https://www.pewresearch.org/fact-tank/2019/07/03/on-average-older-adults-spend-over-half-their-waking-hours-alone/. July 3, 2019.

31 Robert D. Putnam, *Bowling Alone: America's Declining Social Capital* (New York: Palgrave Macmillan, 2000), 178.

32 Americans Oppose Religious Exemptions From Coronavirus-Related Restrictions. Pew Research Center. https://www.pewresearch.org/religion/2020/08/07/americans-oppose-religious-exemptions-from-coronavirus-related-restrictions/. August 7, 2020.

33 Matthew Pressman, "Ambivalent Accomplices: How the Press Handled FDR's Disability and How FDR Handled the Press," *Journal of the Historical Society* 13, no. 3 (2013): 325–59.

34 James P. Pfiffner, "Sexual Probity and Presidential Character," *Presidential Studies Quarterly* 28, no. 4 (1998): 881–86.

35 Virginia A. Chanley, Thomas J. Rudolph, and Wendy M. Rahn, "The Origins and Consequences of Public Trust in Government: A Time Series Analysis," *Public Opinion Quarterly* 64, no. 3 (2000): 239–56.

36 "Public Trust in Government: 1958–2019," Pew Research Center, April 11, 2019, https://tinyurl.com/yxc4g5ok.

37 "Church Allowed Abuse by Priest for Years," *Boston Globe*, January 6, 2002, https://tinyurl.com/j5vpm6y.

38 Lyle E. Larson and Walter Goltz, "Religious Participation and Marital Commitment," *Review of Religious Research* 30, no. 4 (1989): 387–400.

39 Arland Thornton, William G. Axinn, and Daniel H. Hill, "Reciprocal Effects of Religiosity, Cohabitation, and Marriage," *American Journal of Sociology* 98, no. 3 (1992): 628–51.

40 Stan L. Albrecht and Marie Cornwall, "Life Events and Religious Change," in *Latter-day Saint Social Life: Social Research on the LDS Church and Its Members* (Provo, UT: Religious Studies Center, Brigham Young University, 1998), 231–52.

CHAPTER 3

1 "Figure MS-2 Median Age at First Marriage: 1890 to Present," United States Census Bureau, https://tinyurl.com/y9gonr3p.

2 Robert S. Erikson and Laura Stoker, "Caught in the Draft: The Effects of Vietnam Draft Lottery Status on Political Attitudes," *American Political Science Review* 105, no. 2 (2011): 221–37, https://tinyurl.com/yxtdqxeu.

3 Mark J. Perry, "Table of the Day: Bachelor's Degrees for the Class of 2016 by Field and Gender. Oh, and the Overall 25.6% Degree Gap for Men!," AEIdeas, June 18, 2018, https://tinyurl.com/y6625xsy.

4 Nikki Graf, Anna Brown, and Eileen Patten, "The Narrowing, but Persistent, Gender Gap in Pay," Fact Tank, Pew Research Center, March 22, 2019, https://tinyurl.com/y49w5sjg.

5 Gretchen Livingston, "The Rise of Single Fathers," Pew Research Center, Social & Demographic Trends, July 2, 2013, https://tinyurl.com/yxvm9lr2.

6 Megan Brenan, "Record-High 56% of U.S. Women Prefer Working to Homemaking," Gallup, October 24, 2019, https://tinyurl.com/y2s2rpje.

7 Ryan P. Jordan, "Race and Religion in the United States," Oxford Research Encyclopedias, published online April 2017, https://tinyurl.com/y6z4y6nm.

8 Larry L. Hunt, "Hispanic Protestantism in the United States: Trends by Decade and Generation," *Social Forces* 77, no. 4 (1999): 1601–24.

9 Jason E. Shelton and Michael O. Emerson, *Blacks and Whites in Christian America: How Racial Discrimination Shapes Religious Convictions* (New York: NYU Press, 2012).

10 Janelle S. Wong, *Immigrants, Evangelicals, and Politics in an Era of Demographic Change* (New York: Russell Sage Foundation, 2018).

CHAPTER 4

1 Thomas Henry Huxley, letter to Charles A. Watts (publisher of the *Agnostic Annual*), 1883, in *Life and Letters of Thomas Henry Huxley* (London: Macmillan, 1913), 3:97.

2 Campbell, David E., Geoffrey C. Layman, and John C. Green, *Secular Surge: A New Fault Line in American Politics* (Cambridge UK: Cambridge University Press, 2020), 26.

CHAPTER 6

1 Steve Goldstein, "U.S. Enjoys Best Manufacturing Jobs Growth of the Last 30 Years," Market Watch, January 4, 2019, https://tinyurl.com/y4jlprwp.

2 Drew Desilver, "For Most U.S. Workers, Real Wages Have Barely Budged in Decades," Fact Tank, Pew Research Center, August 7, 2018, https://tinyurl.com/y2ok8x9z.

3 Chris Isidore, "Carrier to Ultimately Cut Some of Jobs Trump Saved," CNN, December 9, 2016, https://tinyurl.com/y3a4fpym.

4 Arezou Rezvani, "You can get a $7,500 tax credit to buy an electric car, but it's really complicated," NPR, August 22, 2022.

5 Claire Cain Miller, Josh Katz, Francesca Paris, and Aatish Bhatia, "Vast New Study Show a Key to Reducing Poverty: More Friendships Between Rich and Poor," *New York Times*, August 1, 2022. https://tinyurl.com/24j2kh8z

6 Paul A. Djupe and Christopher P. Gilbert, *The Prophetic Pulpit: Clergy, Churches, and Communities in American Politics* (Lanham, MD: Rowman & Littlefield, 2003).

7 Kenneth D. Wald, David E. Owen, and Samuel S. Hill, "Churches as Political Communities," *American Political Science Review* 82, no. 2 (1988): 531–48.

Recommended Reading

Armstrong, Karen. *The Case for God*. New York: Knopf, 2009.

    This book has stuck with me ever since I first read it a decade ago. *The Case for God* does a tremendous job of packing thousands of years of religious history into a very accessible and well-researched text. I find great value in thinking about God in a way that differs from my Protestant upbringing, and Karen Armstrong is unmatched in her ability to make the reader think about the concept of the divine from the perspectives of different cultures. Her work has also helped me understand why some people find no benefit in believing in God. Every once in a while, I include an anecdote from this book in my Sunday sermon, which is a testament to her work.

Bellah, Robert N., Richard Madsen, William M. Sullivan, Ann Swidler, and Stephen M. Tipton. *Habits of the Heart: Individualism and Commitment in American Life*. With a new preface. Berkeley: University of California, 2007.

    If one were to take a graduate-level survey course on American religion, I am certain that *Habits of the Heart* would be on the syllabus. Robert Bellah and his colleagues conducted in-depth interviews with two hundred research subjects to try to get a sense of what spirituality means in contemporary America. The authors confront a unique facet of American life: our rugged individualism. Their research tries to understand how that predisposition toward personal satisfaction either hinders or enhances the spiritual life of the average citizen. The authors believe that as American society has become fractured, so has religion in the country. As Americans have disconnected from other people, they have drifted away from a belief in the divine.

Or, said another way, social isolation and spiritual isolation are deeply related.

Berlinerblau, Jacques. *Secularism: The Basics*. Abingdon, UK: Routledge, 2021.

Secularism may be one of the most fought over concepts among sociologists who study religion. Despite the fact that it is one of the foundational ideas in social science, it's an incredibly hard term to pin down and often takes on various forms depending on who is using the word. Berlinerblau offers a lucid, concise introduction to secularism in its various forms throughout the pages of this textbook. The real contribution is how the author traces the various schools of thought regarding secularism over the last hundred years, helping readers to have a broader understanding of what the word may mean from a variety of starting points. The book also contains a glossary, a series of case studies, and a terrific collection of sources for further reading for those who are more interested in the philosophical roots of secularism.

Campbell, David E., Geoffrey C. Layman, and John C. Green. *Secular Surge: A New Fault Line in American Politics*. Cambridge, UK: Cambridge University Press, 2020.

Campbell, Layman, and Green are some of the most well-published and well-respected scholars in the field of religion and politics, and in their newest book, they take aim squarely at the rise of nones using a tremendous amount of institutional resources. The primary contribution of the book is the author's ability to tease apart a critical difference in the nones: nonreligious versus secular. The authors contend that atheists and agnostics have not just abandoned a religious perspective, they have replaced it with a secularist/humanist paradigm. On the other hand, a significant portion of nones are not secular—they are merely nonreligious. That is, they have rejected the trappings of religion but have not chosen anything to replace that worldview. Using several proprietary datasets along with some fascinating experiments, Campbell, Layman, and Green significantly advance the way that scholars think about secularism and nonreligion in the United States. For those who want a more academically focused examination of the nones, this book is a tremendous resource.

Putnam, Robert D. *Bowling Alone: The Collapse and Revival of American Community*. Revised and updated. New York: Simon & Schuster, 2020.

This book is the one I bring up most often in interviews, speeches, and presentations when talking about the changes in American society since the 1950s. *Bowling Alone* may be the most widely read political science book published in my lifetime—and for good reason. In astonishing detail, Robert Putnam notes how American society has become fractured and disjointed. People don't meet for social gatherings—for example, by joining bowling leagues—as much as they used to. The book was published two decades ago, so Putnam's assertion that cable television has led to a lot of the social isolation we are experiencing seems quaint now, but the general thesis of the book still rings true today: technology can drive people apart.

Putnam, Robert D., and David E. Campbell. *American Grace: How Religion Divides and Unites Us.* New York: Simon & Schuster, 2010.

Robert Putnam might be the most widely read political scientist alive today, and when he teamed up with one of the preeminent scholars of American religion, David Campbell, they put together a book that is essential reading for those who are interested in long-term trends in American religion. This book excels in weaving together survey data with case studies that focus on interesting ways in which religion has shaped American society. I often assign this text to bring my students up to speed on what has happened in American evangelicalism since the 1970s.

Smietana, Bob. *Reorganized Religion: The Reshaping of the American Church and Why It Matters.* Brentwood, TN: Worthy Publishing. 2022.

Bob Smietana is one of the most well-respected religion journalists in the United States because of his long history of covering denominations, leaders, and movements with the utmost respect and eye toward impartiality. In this book, Smietana takes on an important thought experiment: what will the United States look like when thousands of churches close over the next few decades? He uses a series of case studies of religious organizations who provide tremendous social services to their local community and forces the reader to consider who will fill the gap when those houses of worship close their doors. Smietana's book should serve as an early warning about what the decline of religion will mean to the fabric of the United States. There are implications of this shift that most of us have not even begun to consider.

White, James Emery. *The Rise of the Nones: Understanding and Reaching the Religiously Unaffiliated*. Grand Rapids, MI: Baker, 2014.
This book is one of the earliest to describe the rise of the religiously unaffiliated. James Emery White is a full-time pastor, and therefore, this book is written with a tone and purpose different from many academic books. White does a terrific job of helping fellow religious leaders understand the broad contours of the nones in American society. His book is practical in its approach and includes resources such as discussion questions at the end of each chapter as well as concrete advice for those who are interested in evangelizing the religiously unaffiliated.

Wuthnow, Robert. *Inventing American Religion: Polls, Surveys, and the Tenuous Quest for a Nation's Faith*. Oxford UK: Oxford University Press, 2015.
Robert Wuthnow is one of the giants in the field of the sociology of religion, having authored a number of the seminal pieces in the field. In his later years, he has taken a more reflective tone, and *Inventing American Religion* made me think deeply about a central question: What if all quantitative attempts to study American religion are inaccurate? Obviously, I don't buy Wuthnow's entire argument, but he goes to great lengths to point out some of the issues with the polling industry. If academia has taught me anything, it's to second-guess myself, and this book does a good job of sowing seeds of doubt.